The New York Times

GREAT LATIN SONGS

Library of Congress Catalog Card Number: 73-90174
International Standard Book Number: 8129-0377-3

Photos courtesy of:
**MCA Artists, Ltd.; Leo Griedman; McFadden Strauss Irwin;
Kolling, Lehker and Toy, Inc.,; The Spanish National Tourist Office.**

Music autography by: **Music Art Co.**
Music proofreading by: **Frank Metis**
Jacket and interior design by: **Jerry Lieberman**

The New York Times

GREAT LATIN SONGS

Edited by Richard Broderick
Introduction by Jose Feliciano

QUADRANGLE/THE NEW YORK TIMES BOOK CO.

ALICANTE

MADRID

VALEN (RCA)

LECUONA CUBAN BOYS

LOS CANASTEROS

XAVIER CUGAT

CORDOBA

PILAR LOPEZ

LOUIS LUCENA (RCA)

ANOZ BROTHERS

TOLEDO

CONTENTS

INTRODUCTION

To define what I call the "Latin instinct" in these few paragraphs is as impossible a task as it is to compile all of the best Latin music within the pages of this single volume.

The flamencos of the Spanish gypsies; the boleros of Brazil; the Peruvian valses; the milongas and tangos of Argentina; Venezuela's Guaparos; the Afro-Cuban influence on the Caribbean's calypsos, merengues and salsas; the rancheros of Mexico—Latin music is above all else characterized by its versatility.

Thanks to the early successes of musicians like Perez Prado, Xavier Cugat, Tito Puente, Desi Arnaz, and many others, all North America was doing the mambo, the samba, the cha cha cha and the bossa nova with an assist by Arthur Murray.

JOSE FELICIANO

The Latin explosion continued with Antonio Carlos Jobim, Sergio Mendes, Herb Alpert, Trini Lopez and a host of others as Americans clamored for more and more of *that* sound. And more they got. There was even a young Puerto Rican lad who added a little of his own fuel to the fire. Latin music came into its own. It emerged—or so it seemed to non-Latins—as a major force in the popular music field. Contemporary musicians were quick to latch on to this new musical bonanza that was selling millions of records. Before long everyone had at least one "Latin" album.

Today, Latin music has emerged and come out of a strictly Latin "bag," making the transition into virtually every phase of contemporary music from Santana and Mongo Santamaria to Elton John and Carole King.

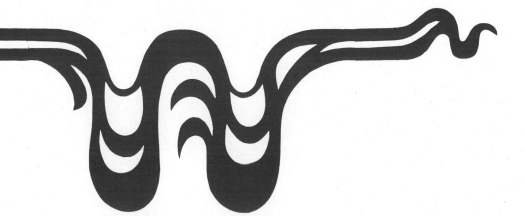

JOSE FELICIANO

ADIOS VIDA MIA

English lyrics by Joe Davis
Spanish lyrics by Francisco Cepeda C.
Music by Jesus Martinez G.

Moderately, with expression

Chorus:

Good-bye, Lit - tle Dar - ling, _____ I say fare-well to you; _____
A - dios vi - da mí - a, _____ me ven-go a des - pe - dir, _____

Good-bye, Lit - tle Dar - ling, _____ This time I'm real - ly through. _____
sé bien que tu pe - cho _____ no sus - pi - ra por mí; _____

I'm sor - ry to leave you,_____ But what else can I do?
A - dios i - lu - sio - nes_____ ya no vol - ve - ré_a - mar,

I thought some day you'd kiss me and say that you love me the way I love
Y sin tu_a - mor, bien mí - o la flor de mi vi - da se va_a mar - chi -

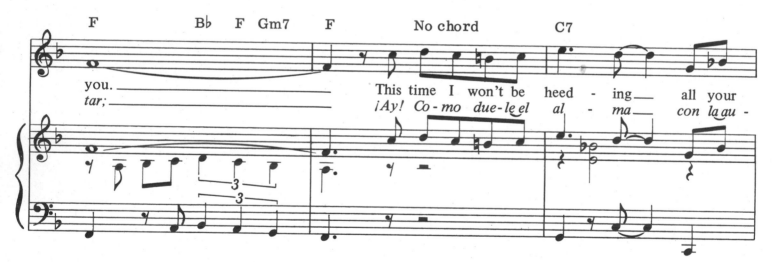

you._____ This time I won't be heed - ing_____ all your
tar;_____ ¡Ay! Co - mo due - le_el al - ma_____ con la_au -

plead - ing,_____ Let's be fair, dear;_____ My heart I'd be de -
sen - cia_____ de_un ca - ri - ño,_____ Los pa - ja - ros no

ADIOS

English lyrics by Eddie Woods
Spanish lyrics and music by Enric Madriguera

Verse:

We were so hap - py, dear,___ to - geth - er,___ And ev - 'ry
Ya la a - le - grí - a de___ mi vi - da___ Es co - mo un

dream of joy___ we knew,___ A cas - tle in the air,___ dear, for -
sue - ño que se vá___ por - que al lle - gar de nue - vo el

ev - er,___ A world of love for just___ we two.___ But ev - 'ry
di - a___ con mi i - lu - sión me he dea - le - jar.___ Por e - so

dream must have___ its end - ing,___ Our cas - tle falls and we___ must part___
ven - go has - ta___ tu re - ja___ A des - pe - dir - me dul - ce a - mor___

___ So, dear, this mes - sage to___ you I'm send - ing,___ A word of
___ Por e - so mi al - ma tris - te se que - ja___ cuan - do a - sí

hope, from my___ ach - ing heart.
te can - ta___ su do - lor.

Smoothly

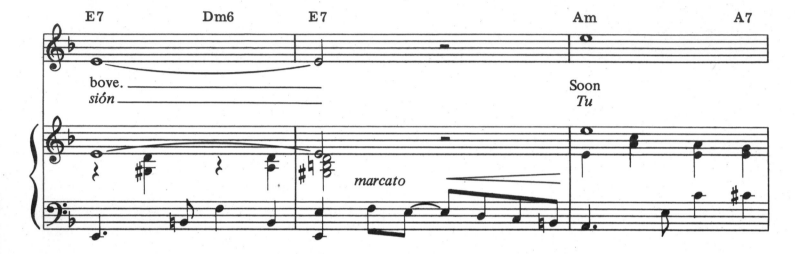

24

Always in My Heart

English lyrics by Kim Gannon
Spanish lyrics and music by Ernesto Lecuona

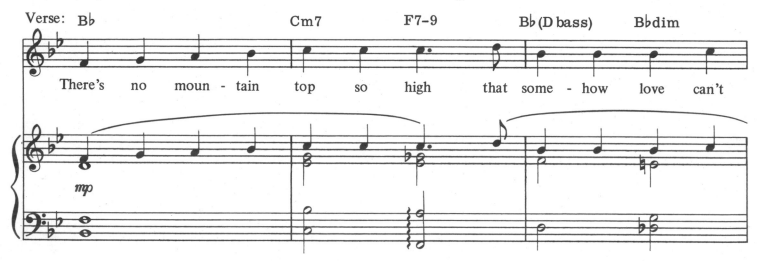

Verse:
There's no moun-tain top so high that some-how love can't

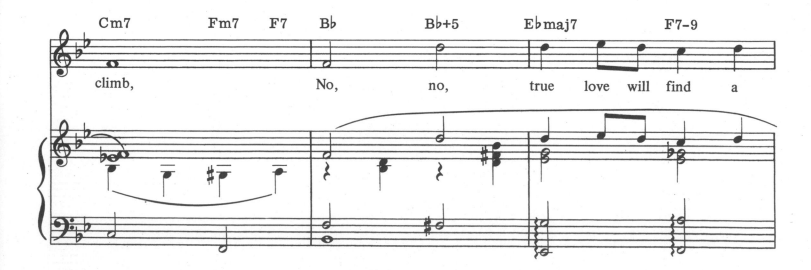

climb, No, no, true love will find a

way.

There's no riv - er

quite so wide That love can't cross in time,

Please be - lieve me when I say:

Slowly, with expression

Chorus: No chord

You are Al - ways In My Heart
Siem - pre es - tá en mi co - ra - zón

27

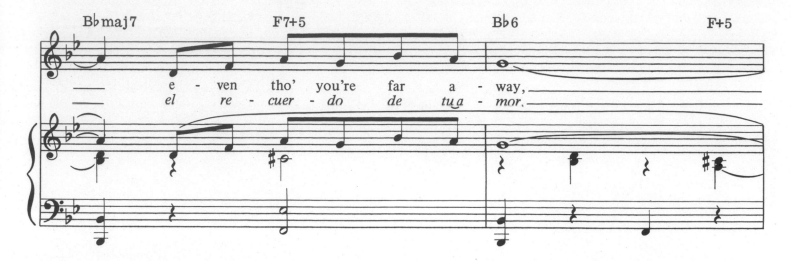

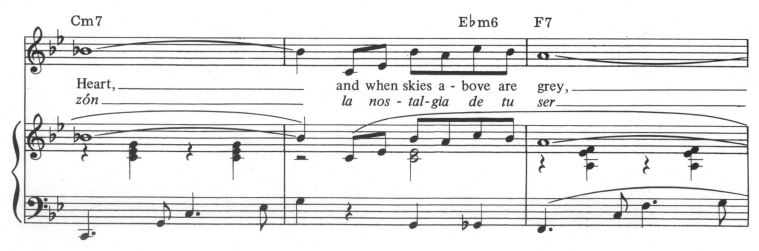

Cm7

I re-mem-ber that you care____ and then and
y a ho - ra pue - do com - pren - der____ qué dul - ce ha

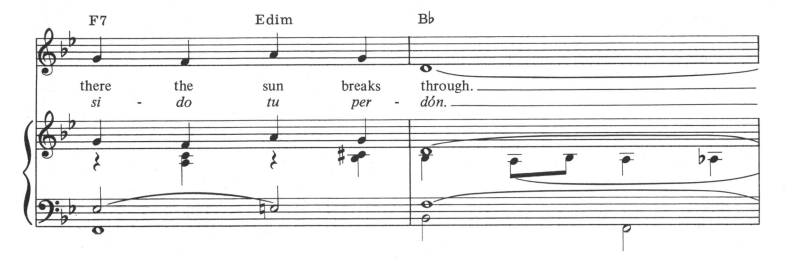

F7 **Edim** **B♭**

there the sun breaks through.____
si - do tu per - dón.____

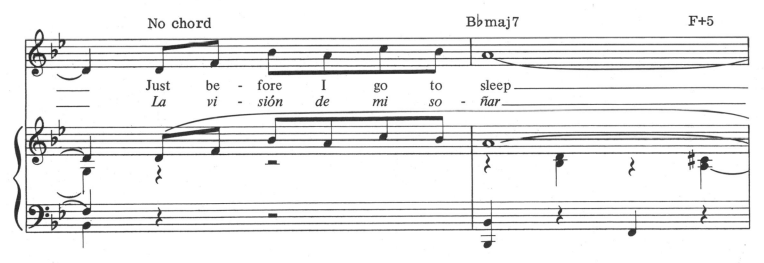

No chord **B♭maj7** **F+5**

Just be - fore I go to sleep____
La vi - sión de mi so - ñar____

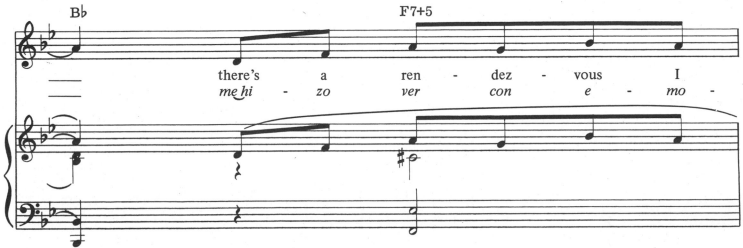

B♭ **F7+5**

there's a ren - dez - vous I
me hi - zo ver con e - mo -

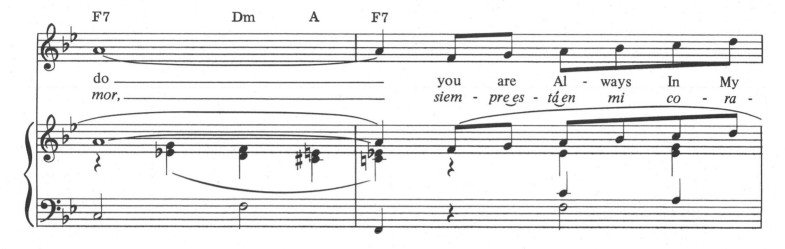

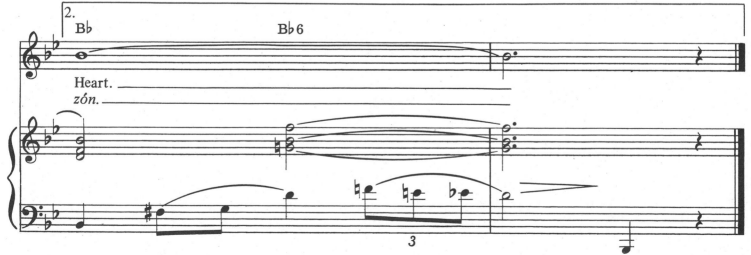

AMAPOLA

English lyrics by Albert Gamse
Spanish lyrics and music by Joseph M. Lacalle

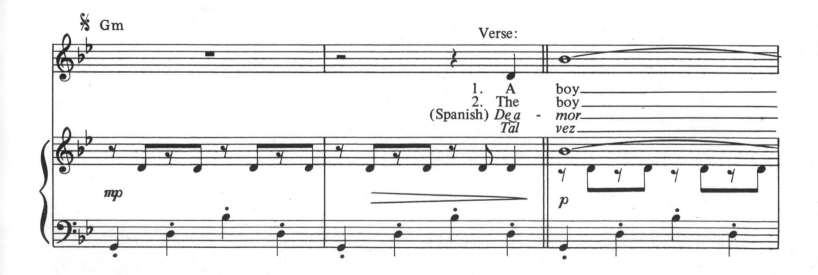

found a dream up-on a dis - tant   shore,
left his love up-on a dis - tant   shore,
en los hie - rros de tu re - ja
en los hie - rros de tu re - ja

A maid   with a way of whis-p'ring
And sailed   from the one his arms were
De a - mor   *es - cu - ché la tris - te*
Trai - dor   *el a - mor sin - tió su*

"si se - ñor."   Each night
long - ing for.   He vowed
que - ja   *De a - mor*
que - ja   *A - mor*

Gm

while gui - tars would soft - ly play,
he'd re - turn one sun - ny day,
que so - ñó en mi co - ra - zón
que en mi a - man - te co - ra - zón

D

The tune seemed to dance
Once more to re - peat
Di - cién - do - me a - sí
Sem - bró por mi mal

A7   **D**   **F7**

'round the words that he'd say:
what his heart had to say:
con su dul - ce can - ción
u - na dul - ce i - lu - sión

poco rit.

Chorus:

A - ma - po - la, _____ my pret - ty lit - tle
A - ma - po - la _____ lin - di - si - ma A - ma -

pop - py, _____ You're like that love - ly flow'r so
po - la _____ Se - rá siem - pre mi al - ma

sweet and heav - en - ly _____ Since I
tu - ya so - la _____ Yo te

found you, _____ My heart is wrapped a - round you _____
quie - ro _____ a - ma - da ni - ña mi - a _____

And lov - ing you, it seems to beat a
I - gual que_a - ma la flor la luz del

B♭

rhap - so - dy._____ A - ma - po - la,_____
di - a_____ A - ma - po - la_____

the pret - ty lit - tle pop - py_____
lin - di - si - ma_A - ma - po - la_____

G7   **Dm7**   **G7**

must cop - y its en - dear - ing charm from
No se_a tan in - gra - ta y á - ma -

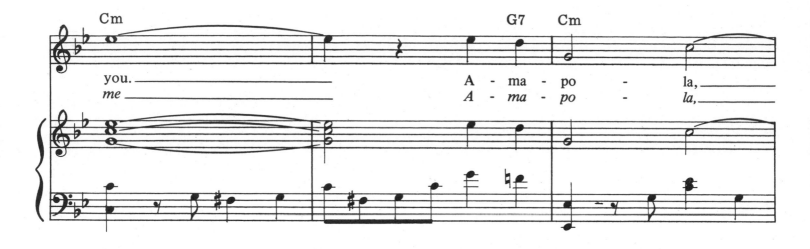

AMOR

English lyrics by Sunny Skylar
Spanish lyrics by Ricardo Lopez Mendez
Music by Gabriel Ruiz

Beguine

mor,_____ This word so sweet that I re-
mor,_____ Na - ció de tí, Na - ció de

G7

peat Means I a - dore you._____ A -
mí, de la es - pe - ran - za._____ A -

Dm

mor, A - mor, my love,_____
mor, A - mor, A - mor,_____

G7

___ Would you de - ny this heart that I Have placed be -
___ Na - ció de Dios, pa - ra los dos, Na - ció del

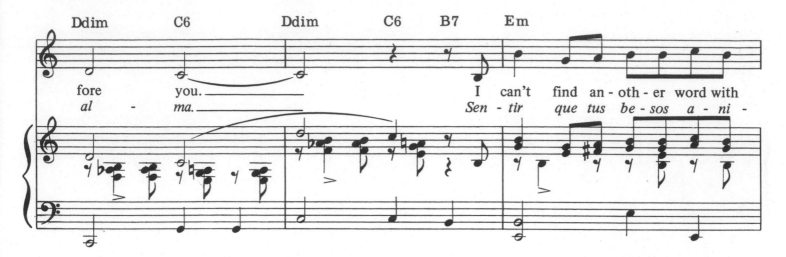

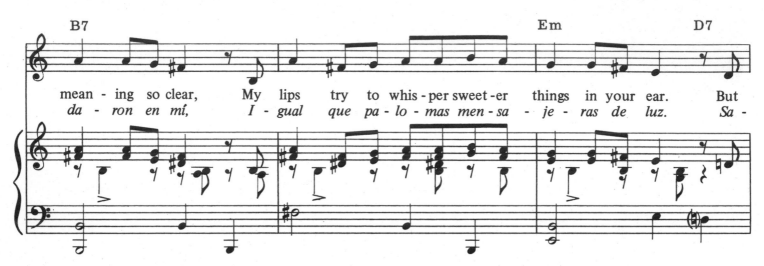

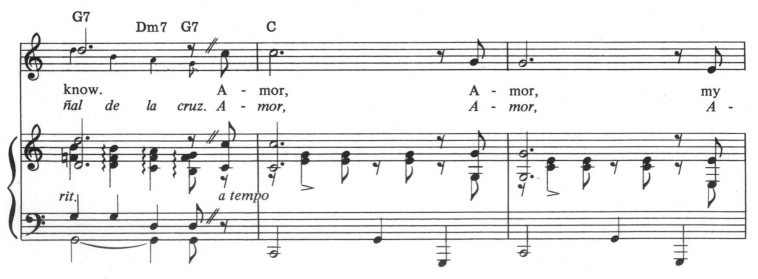

love,_____ When you're a - way there is no
mor_____ Na - ció de tí, Na - ció de

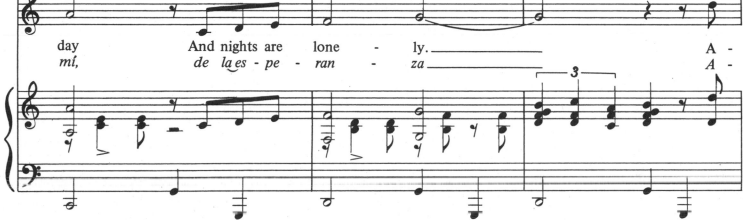

G7

day And nights are lone - ly._____ A -
mí, de la es - pe - ran - za_____ A -

Dm

mor, A - mor, my love,
mor, A - mor, A - mor,

G7 | **1.**

Make life di - vine, Say you'll be mine, And love me
Na - ció de Dios, pa - ra los dos, Na - ció del

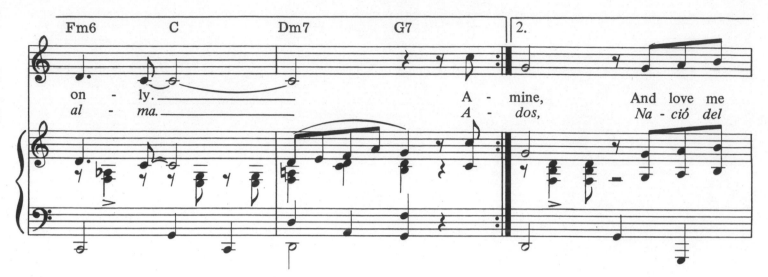

on - ly. _____
al - ma. _____

A - mine, And love me
A - dos, Na - ció del

on - ly, _____
al - ma, _____

A -
A -

mor, _____
mor, _____

A - mor. _____
A - mor. _____

poco a poco cresc.

ff

gva.
gliss.

BABALÚ

English lyrics by S.K. Russell
Spanish lyrics and music by Margarita Lecuona

Slow and Barbaric

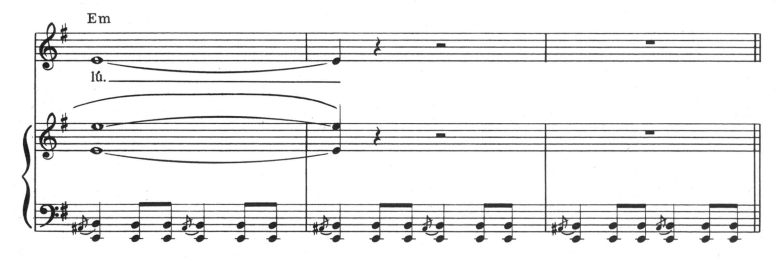

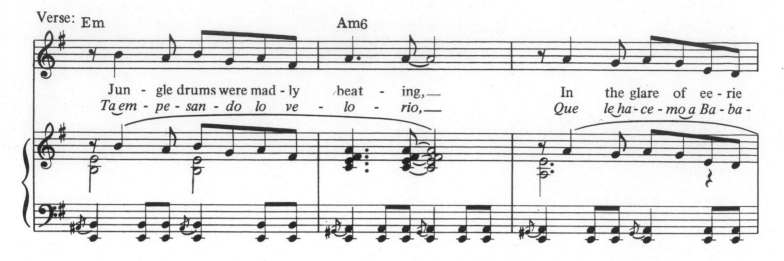

Verse:

Jun - gle drums were mad - ly beat - ing,___ In the glare of ee - rie
Ta em - pe - san - do lo ve - lo - rio,___ Que le ha - ce - mo a Ba - ba-

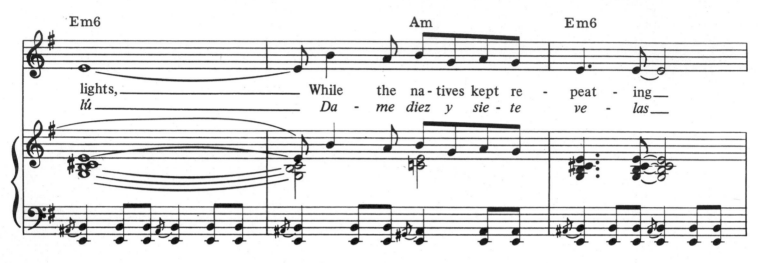

lights,___ While the na - tives kept re - peat - ing___
lú___ Da - me diez y sie - te ve - las___

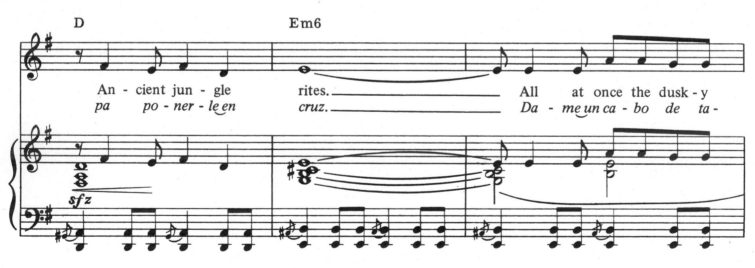

An - cient jun - gle rites.___ All at once the dusk - y
pa po - ner - le en cruz.___ Da - me un ca - bo de ta-

war - ri - ors be - gan to___ raise their arms to skies a - bove,___
ba - co ma - yen - ye___ y un ja - rri - to de a-guar - dien - te___

44

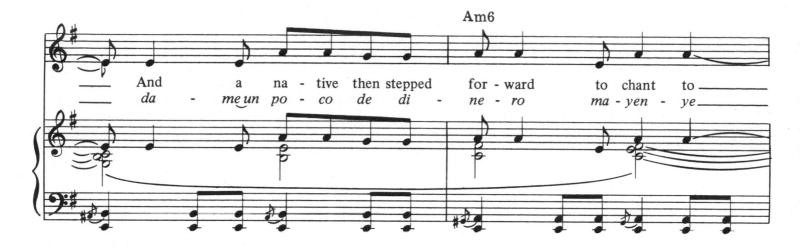

And a na-tive then stepped for-ward to chant to _____
da - me un po - co de di - ne - ro ma - yen - ye _____

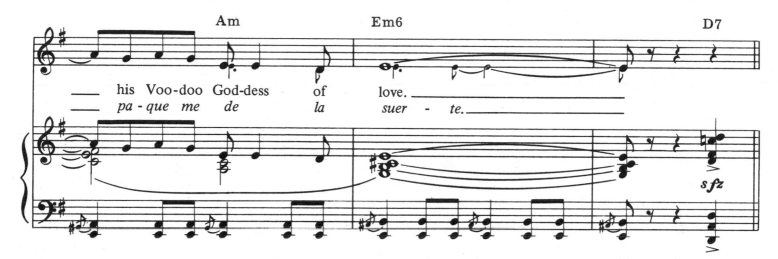

_____ his Voo-doo God-dess of love. _____
pa - que me de la suer - te. _____

Chorus:

Ah! great Ba - ba - lú! _____ I'm so lost and for - e -
Yo quie - re pe - dí que mi ne - gra me

sak - en _____ Ah! great Ba - ba - lú _____
quie - ra _____ Que ten - ga di - ne - ro _____

Bring back the love you've tak - en.
y que no se mue - ra.

You can re - store all the dreams that once were mine If
Ay! yo le quie - ro pe - dí A Ba - ba - lú 'na

on - ly you'll use some mys - tic sign. Ah! great Ba - ba - lú!
ne - gra muy san - ta co - mo tú Que no ten - ga o - tro ne - gro

Bring her back to me; Ah!
pa - que no se fue - ra.

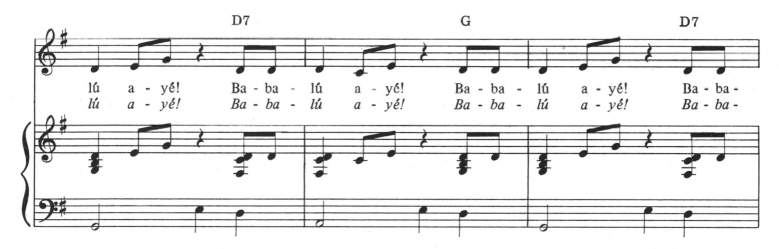

BE MINE TONIGHT

English lyrics by Sunny Skylar
Music by Maria Teresa Lara

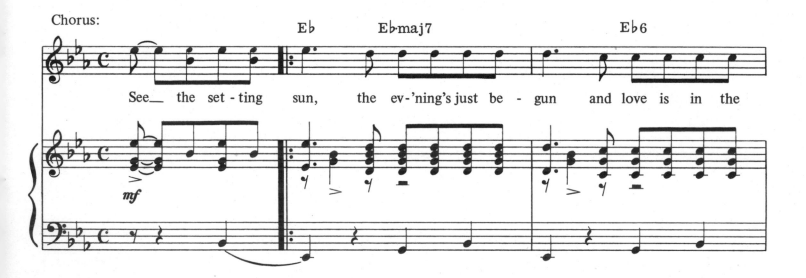

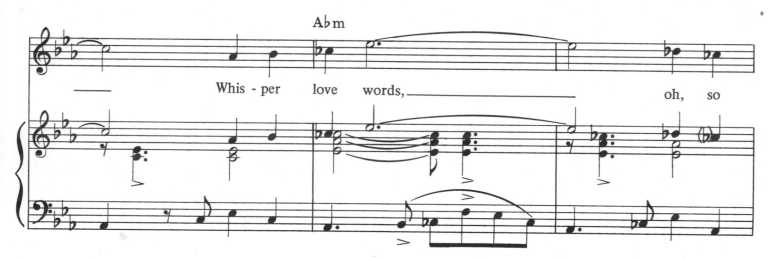

BESAME MUCHO

English lyrics by Sunny Skylar
Spanish lyrics and music by Consuelo Velazquez

Moderately

Chorus:

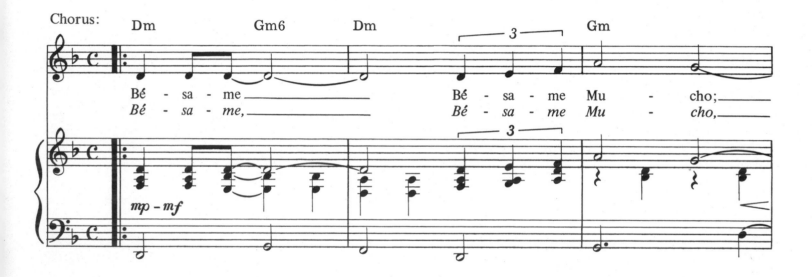

Bé - sa - me _____ Bé - sa - me Mu - cho; _____
Bé - sa - me, _____ Bé - sa - me Mu - cho, _____

Each time I cling to your kiss I hear mu - sic di -
co - mo si fue - ra es - ta no - che la úl - ti - ma

Nev - er knew this thrill be - fore; Who ev - er thought I'd be
o - jos, *ver - te jun - to a mí,* *pien - sa que tal vez ma -*

hold - ing you close to me, Whisp - 'ring, "It's you I a - dore;"
ña - na yo ya es - ta - ré *le - jos, muy le - jos de ti.*

Dear - est one,_____ if you should leave me,_____
Bé - sa - me,_____ *Bé - sa - me Mu - cho,_____*

_____ Each lit - tle dream would take wing and my life would be
co - mo si fue - ra es - ta no - che la úl - ti - ma

Brazil

English lyrics by S.K. Russell
Music by Ary Barroso

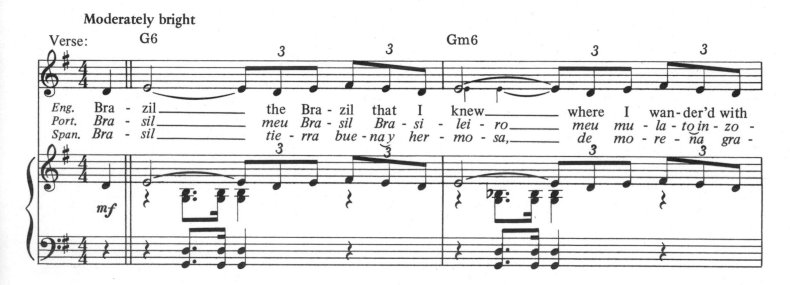

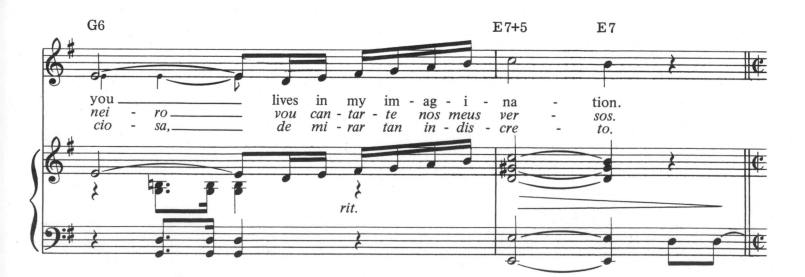

Where the songs are pas-sion-ate, And a smile has flash_in it,
O Bra - sil, sam - ba_que da, bam - bo - leio, Que faz_gin - ga,
¡Oh, Bra - sil, ver - de_que da, pa - ra el mun - do ad - mi - rar,

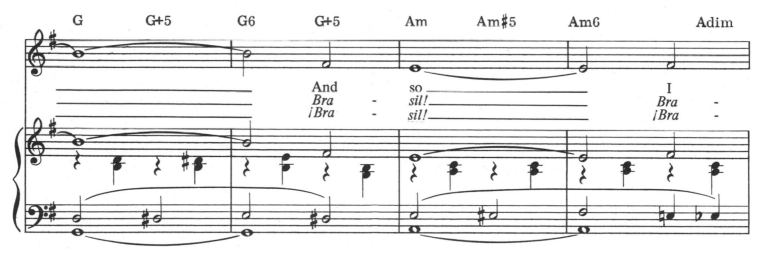

And a kiss has art_in it, For you put your heart_in it,___
O Bra - sil, do meu a - mor, Ter - ra de nos - so_Sen - hor,_
el Bra - sil, de mi a - mor, tie - rra de nues - tro_Se - ñor!_

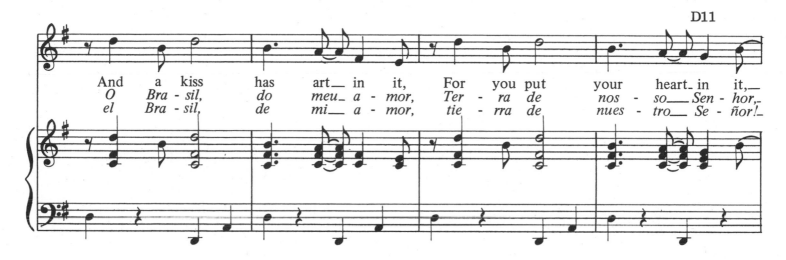

And so___ I
Bra - sil!___ Bra -
¡Bra - sil!___ ¡Bra -

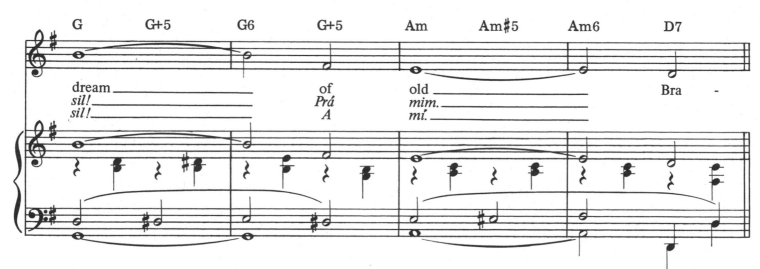

dream___ of old___ Bra -
sil!___ Prá mim.___
sil!___ A mí.___

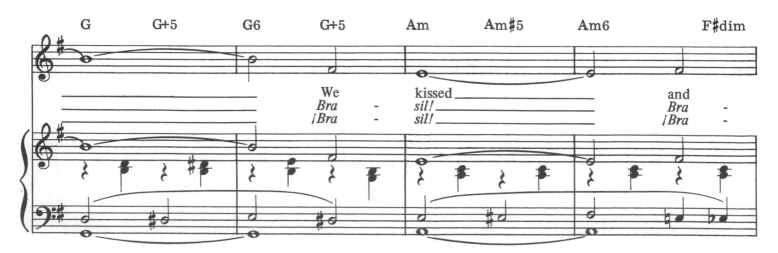

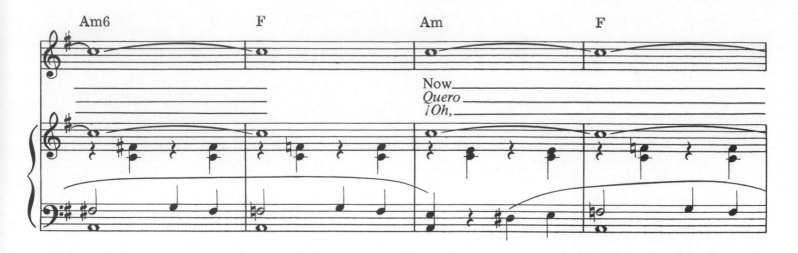

when twi - light dims the sky a - bove, _____
_ ver a "sa do - na" ca - mi - nhan - do,_____
_ e - se Bra - sil lin - do y mo - re - no,_____

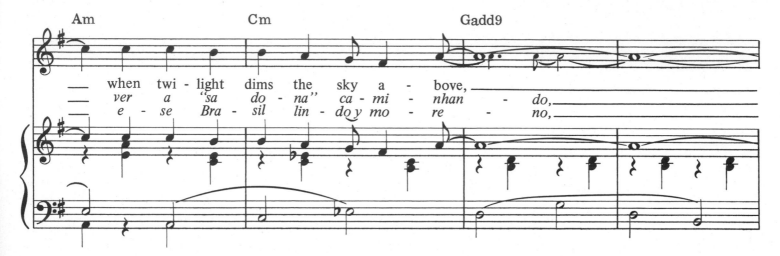

_ Re - call - ing thrills of our love,_____
Pe - los sa - lões ar - ras - tan - do,_____
es el Bra - sil bra - si - le - ro,_____

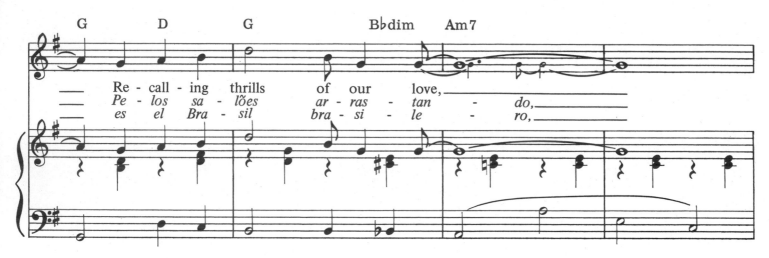

There's one thing I'm cer - tain of: _____ Re -
O seu ves - ti - do ren - da - do,_____ Bra -
tie - rra de sam - ba y can - cio - nes! _____ ¡Bra -

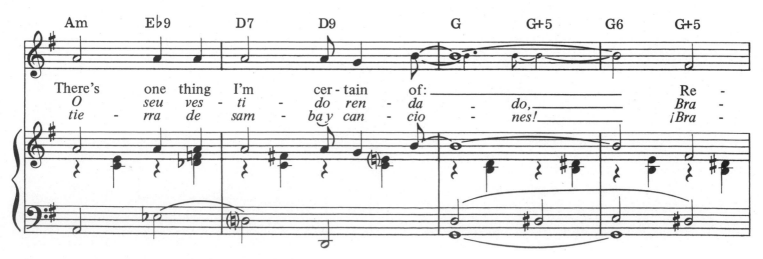

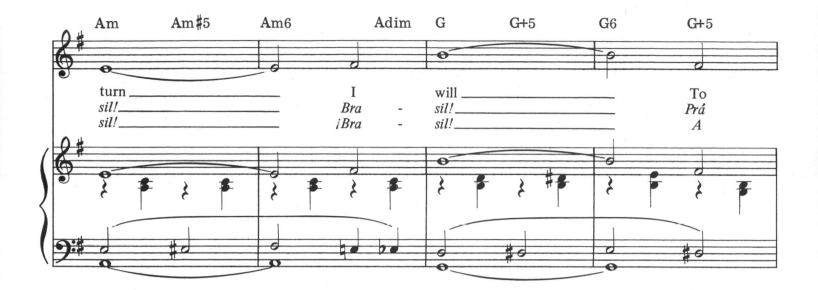

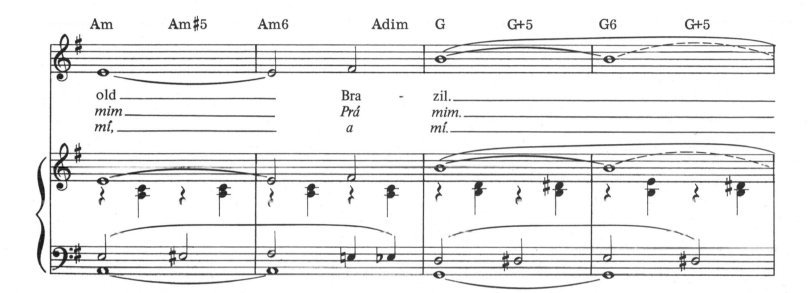

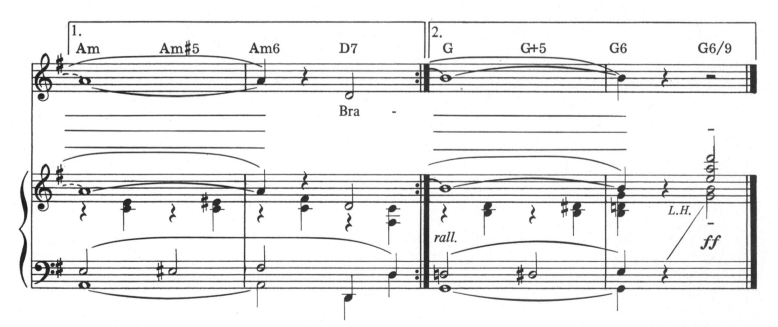

THE BREEZE AND I

Lyrics by Al Stillman
Music by Ernesto Lecuona

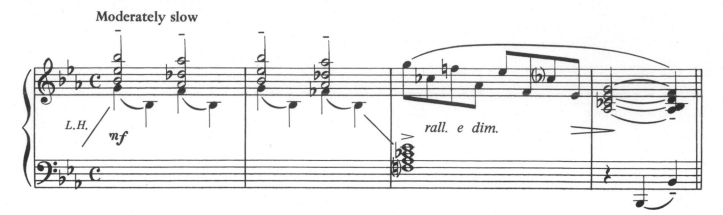

COSE, COSE, COSE

Words and music by Joe Davis and Armando Castro

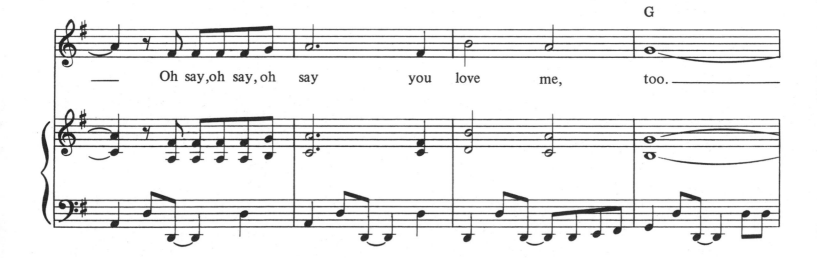

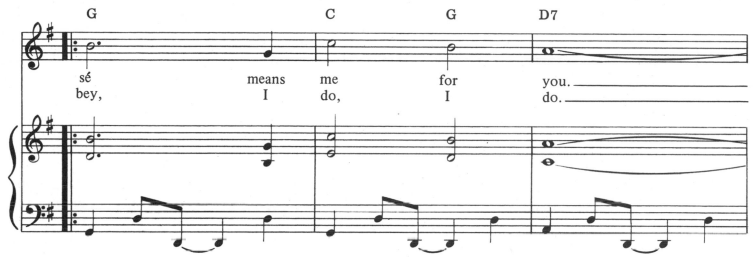

THE CONSTANT RAIN

English lyrics by Norman Gimbel
Portuguese lyrics and music by Jorge Ben

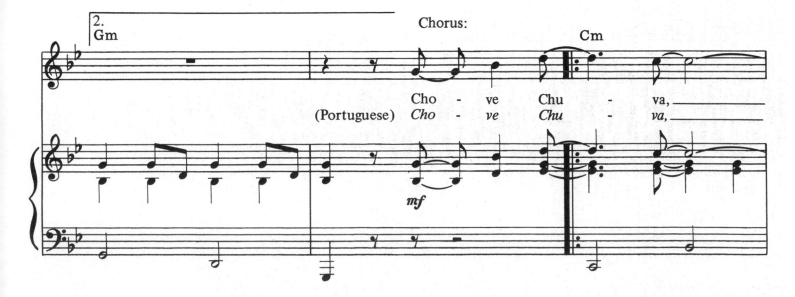

Con - stant is the rain.____
cho - ve sem pa - rar.____
Cho - ve Chu-
Cho - ve Chu-

va,____
va,____
End - less is the pain.____
cho - ve sem pa - rar.____

As I stand here and re - mem - ber____
Pois eu fa - zer u - ma pre - ce
That once, our____ hearts were
Pra Deus nos - so Se -

one ____
nhor ____
And ev' - ry day was spring to me,
Pra chu - va____ pa - rar
Till you (he) (she)
De mo -

LA COMPARSA

English lyrics by Albert Gamse
Spanish lyrics and music by Ernesto Lecuona

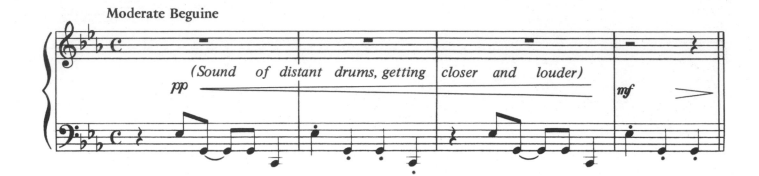

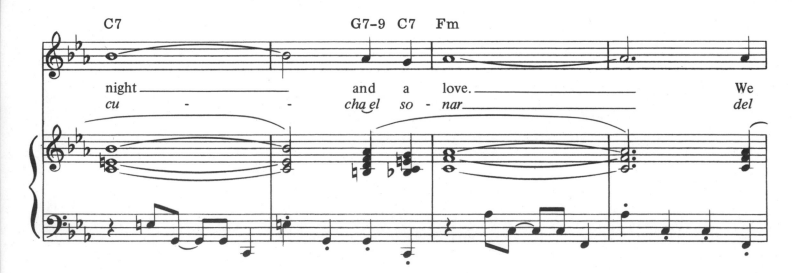

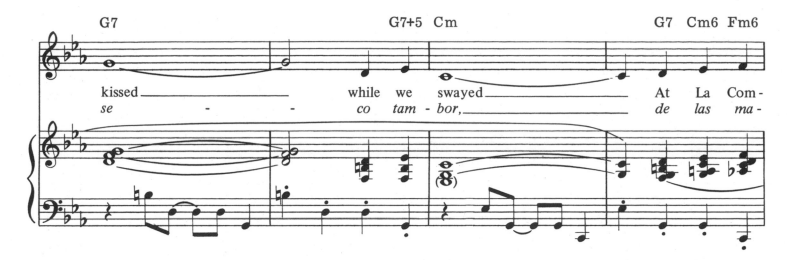

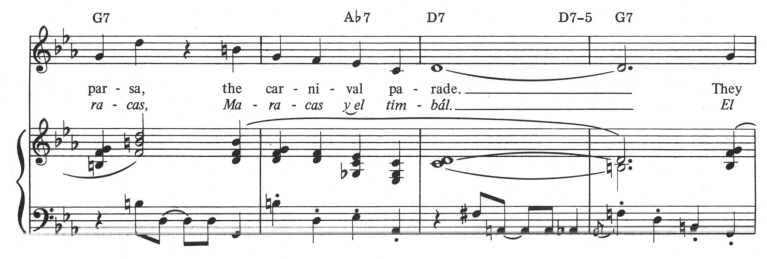

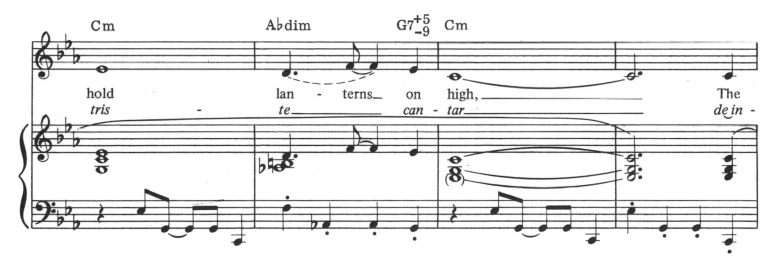

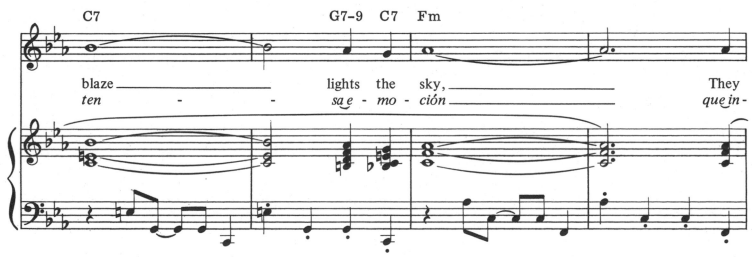

dance_____ through the street,_____ While drums are

vi - - ta a so - nar_____ al a mo -

played with a strange, rhyth - mic beat._____

ro - so___ co - ra - zón._____

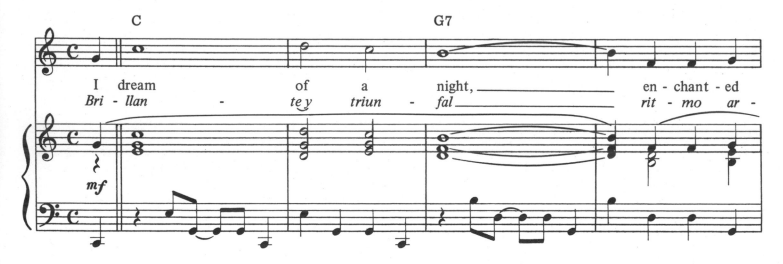

I dream of a night,_____ en - chant - ed

Bri - llan - te y triun - fal_____ rit - mo ar -

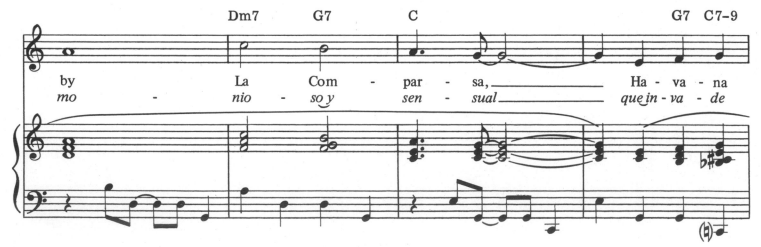

by La Com - par - sa,_____ Ha - va - na

mo - nio - so y sen - sual_____ que in - va - de

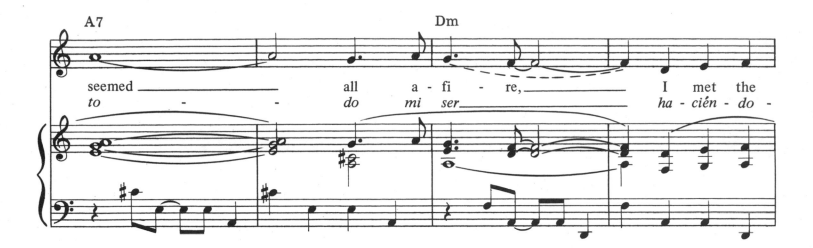

seemed _____ all a-fi-re, _____ I met the
to - - do mi ser _____ ha - cién - do-

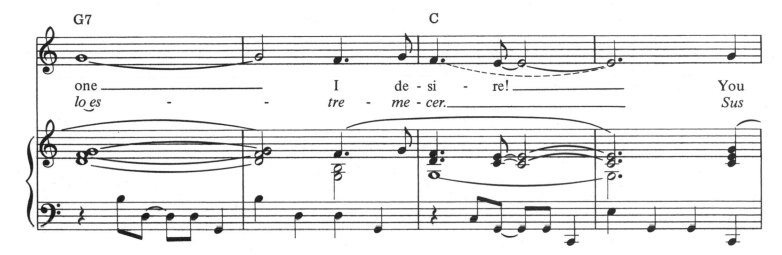

one _____ I de-si-re! _____ You
lo es - - tre - me - cer. _____ Sus

held me, my heart was beat-ing a-loud. We kissed and
má - gi - cos so - nes _____ in - spi-ran

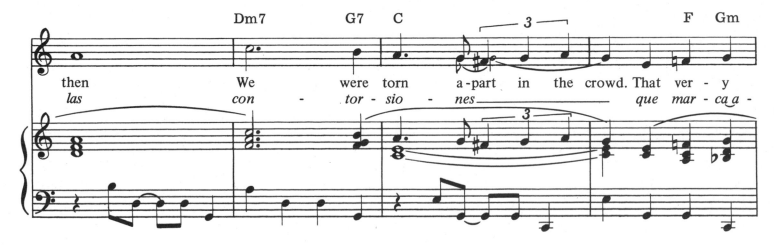

then We were torn a-part in the crowd. That ver-y
las con - tor - sio - nes _____ que mar - ca a-

mo - ment, I lost you,_____ and yet my
si'el bai - la - dor_____ con lú - bri -

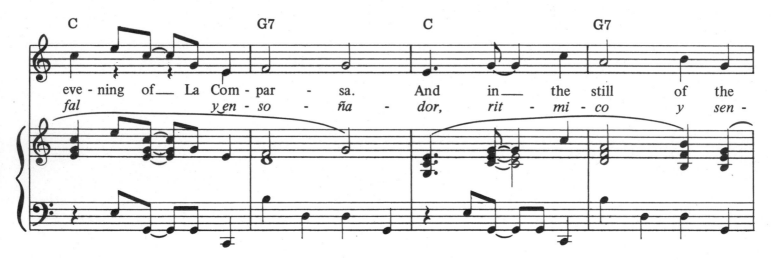

dreams _____ re - store all_ the thrill of the
co _____ fer - vor. Bri - llan - te y tri - un -

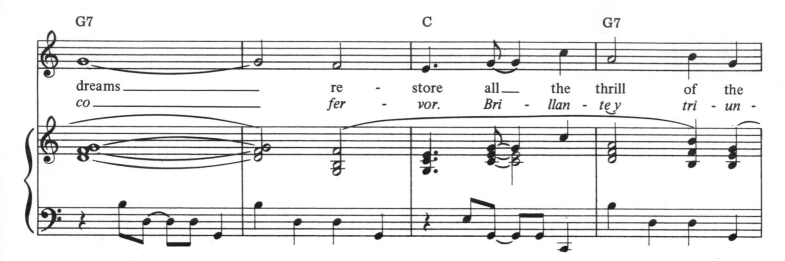

eve - ning of_ La Com - par - sa. And in_ the still of the
fal y en - so - ña - dor, rit - mi - co y sen -

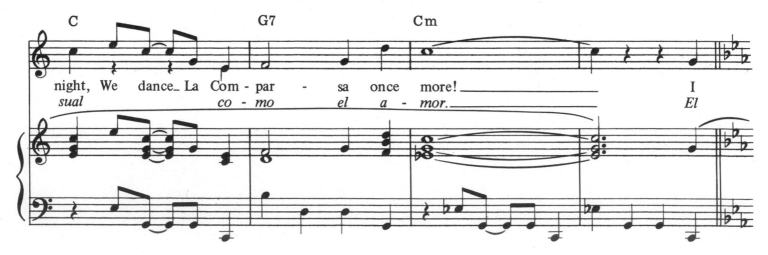

night, We dance_ La Com - par - sa once more! _____ I
sual co - mo el a - mor._____ El

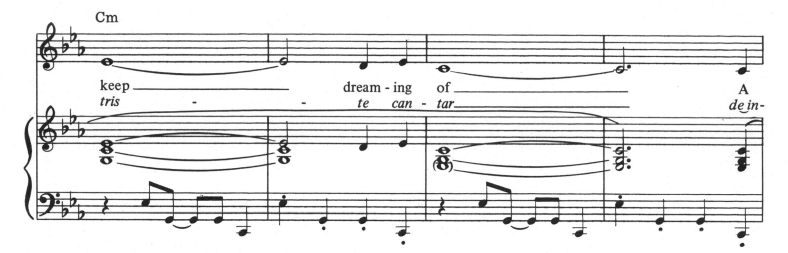

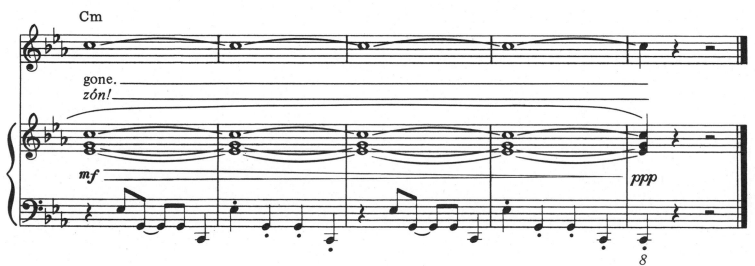

LA CUCARACHA

English lyrics by Stanley Adams
Arranged by Paul Hill

Moderately

mouse, He gets in trou - ble, a lot of trou - ble, Snoop-ing here and ev - 'ry -
mar, La Cu - ca - ra - cha, La Cu - ca - ra - cha, Ya no pue-de ca - mi -

where,_ La Cu-ca - ra - cha, La Cu-ca - ra - cha, Al-ways keeps the cup-board bare.
nar,___Por-que no tie - ne, por-que le fal - ta, Ma - ri - hua - na que fu - mar.

Verse:

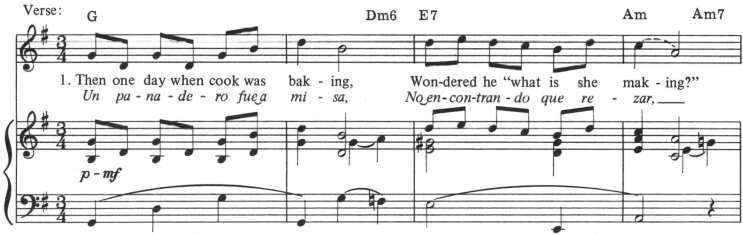

1. Then one day when cook was bak - ing, Won-dered he "what is she mak - ing?"
Un pa - na - de - ro fue a mi - sa, No en-con-tran - do que re - zar,___

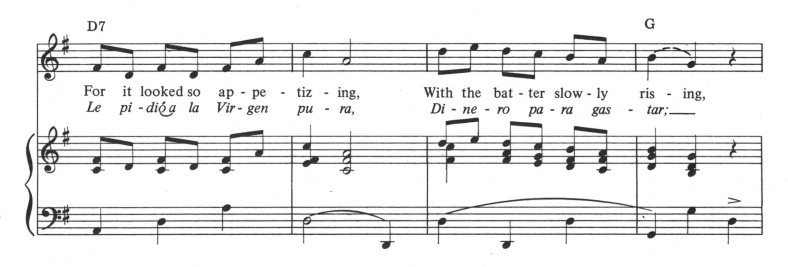

For it looked so ap - pe - tiz - ing, With the bat - ter slow - ly ris - ing,
Le pi - dió a la Vir - gen pu - ra, Di - ne - ro pa - ra gas - tar;___

To the edge he start-ed skip-ping, Then he found that he was slip-ping
Un pa-na-de-ro fue a mi-sa, No en-con-tran-do que re-zar,

In the pie so hot and blaz-in', Now he's just an-oth-er
Le pi-dió a la Vir-gen pu-ra, Di-ne-ro pa-ra gas-

1.2.3.4. **5.**

rai-sin. La Cu-ca- rai-sin. La Cu-ca-ra-cha, La Cu-ca-ra-cha,
tar. La Cu-ca- tar. La Cu-ca-ra-cha, La Cu-ca-ra-cha,

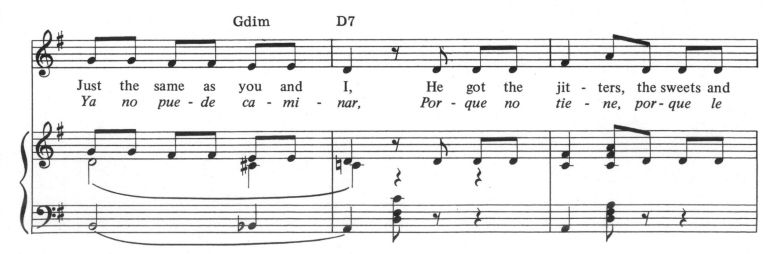

Just the same as you and I, He got the jit-ters, the sweets and
Ya no pue-de ca-mi-nar, Por-que no tie-ne, por-que le

bit - ters, Lived and loved and said "good - bye."
fal - ta, Ma - ri - hua - na que fu - mar.

2.

La Cucaracha, La Cucaracha,
Wandered in a dressing room,
A lovely lady, a pretty lady,
Couldn't see well in the gloom,
La Cucaracha, La Cucaracha,
Fell into her make-up bowl,
When she had painted, she nearly fainted,
Thought her face had grown a mole.

Later on when he was older,
Then he found the nights much colder,
Till he saw a sleeve wide open,
Snug and warm as he was hopin',
'Twas the time and place for napping,
Till somebody started slapping,
Woe betide the little midget,
He had made the owner fidget.

3.

La Cucaracha, La Cucaracha,
Met a little Pekingnese,
La Cucaracha, La Cucaracha,
Bit his nose and made him sneeze,
The little doggie, the little doggie,
Tho' he dug and dug and dug,
La Cucaracha, La Cucaracha,
He was safe beneath a rug.

Then one day when he was thinner,
He just looked around for dinner,
And he tumbled never thinking,
In the soup and started sinking,
Oh the cook began to holler,
Grabbed the butler by the collar,
Out the window went the platter,
But our little friend was fatter.

4.

La Cucaracha, La Cucaracha,
Woke up on election day,
La Cucaracha, La Cucaracha,
Heard the things they had to say,
A lot of lying and alibiing,
Empty heads without a plan,
La Cucaracha, La Cucaracha,
Said, "I'm glad I'm not a man?"

Then one day he saw an army,
Said, "The drums and bugle charm me,
Still if all the world are brothers,
Why should these men fight the others?
Guess it's just for love and glory,
Who'd believe another story?
These are men so brave and plucky,
Look at me, boy am I lucky!"

5.

La Cucaracha, La Cucaracha,
Wondered where his love could be,
La Cucaracha, La Cucaracha,
Wandered on so mis'rably.
The bees and beetles and old boll weevils,
Chased him off with many "Scats,"
First they would scold him and then they told him,
They were bug aristocrats.

Then one day while in the garden,
He just said, "I beg your pardon,"
To a lady Cucaracha,
And he added, "Now I've gotcha."
She was coy but she was willing,
And for years their love was thrilling,
They still meet at half past seven,
Up in Cucaracha heaven.

La Cucaracha, La Cucaracha,
Just the same as you and I,
He got the jitters, the sweets and bitters,
Lived and loved and said "Goodbye."

EL CUMBANCHERO

Lyrics and music by Rafael Hernandez

cum - ba, cum - ba, cum - ba, cum - ban - che - ro.

bon - go, bon - go, bon - go, bon - go - se - ro.

Pri - qui - tí que va so - nan - do el cum - ban -

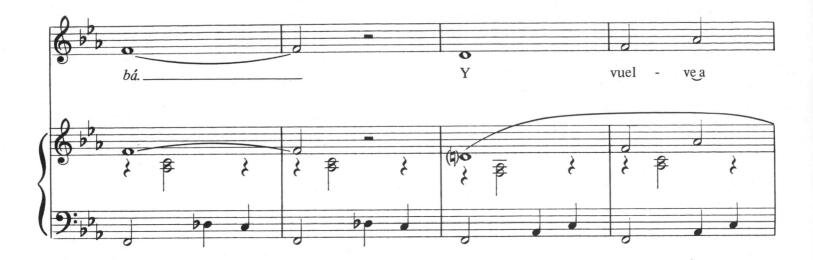

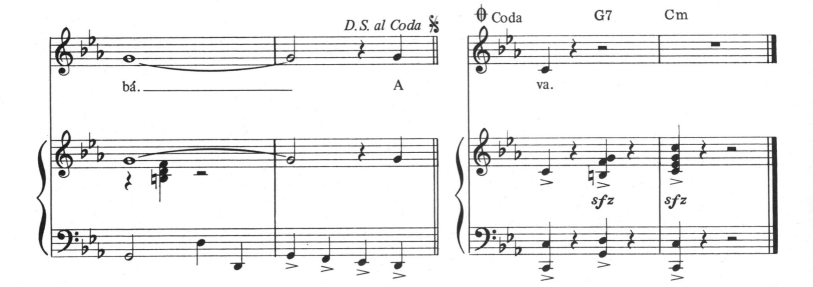

CUANTO LE GUSTA

Lyrics by Ray Gilbert
Music by Gabriel Ruiz

Cuan - to Le Gus - ta, le gus - ta, le gus - ta, le

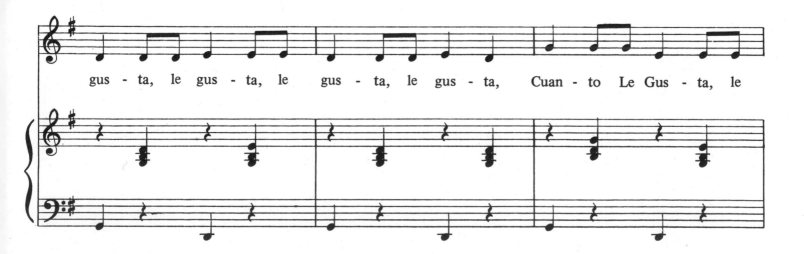

gus - ta, le gus - ta, le gus - ta, le gus - ta, Cuan - to Le Gus - ta, le

gus - ta, le gus - ta, le gus - ta, le gus - ta, le gus - ta.

Chorus:

We got - ta get go - in', where we go - in'? And what - a we gon - na

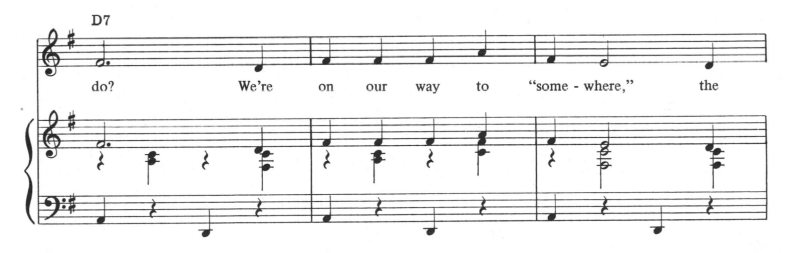

do? We're on our way to "some - where," the

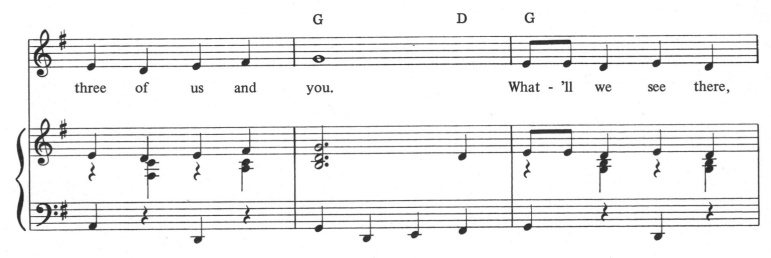

three of us and you. What - 'll we see there,

who will be there, What-'ll be the big sur - prise? There

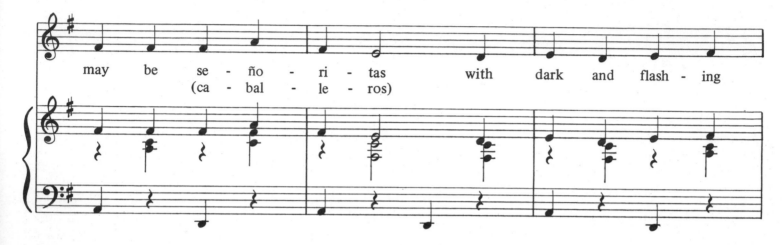

may be se - ño - ri - tas with dark and flash - ing
(ca - bal - le - ros)

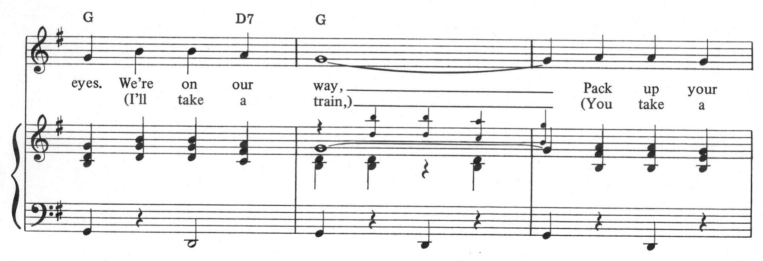

eyes. We're on our way, _____ Pack up your
(I'll take a train,) _____ (You take a

pack, _____ And if we stay, _____
boat,) _____ (I'll take a plane,) _____

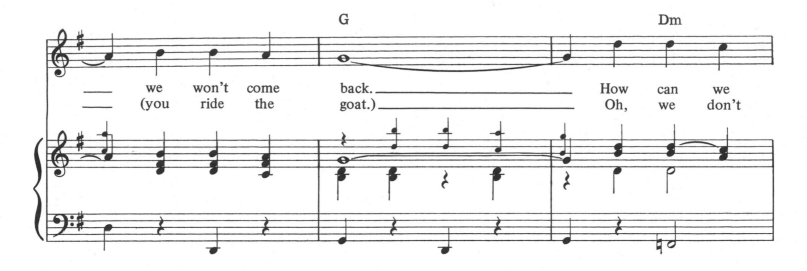

we won't come back. How can we
(you ride the goat.) Oh, we we don't

go, We have - n't got a dime,
care, We'll ei - ther walk or climb,

But we're go - in', And we're gon - na have a hap - py

To Patter

time.

Fine

time.

To Coda

89

place we want to go. _____ We

Coda

Cuan - to Le Gus - ta, le gus - ta, le gus - ta, le

gus - ta, le gus - ta, le gus - ta, le gus - ta, Cuan - to Le Gus - ta, le

gus - ta, le gus - ta, le gus - ta, le gus - ta, le gus - ta.

CU-CU-RRU-CU-CU, PALOMA

English lyrics by Pat Valando and Ronnie Carson
Spanish lyrics and music by Tomas Mendez

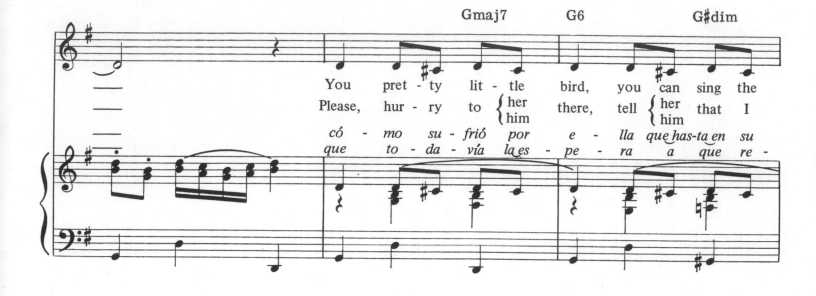

You   pret-ty   lit-tle   bird,   you   can   sing   the
Please,   hur-ry   to { her / him } there,   tell { her / him } that   I
có - mo   su-frió   por   e - lla   que has-ta en   su
que   to - da - vía   la es - pe - ra   a   que   re -

words,   you   can   tell { her / him! } bet - ter._____
care,   tell { her / him } with   your   coo - ing._____
muer - te   la   fué   lla - man - do._____
gre - se   la   des - di - cha - da._____

Chorus:

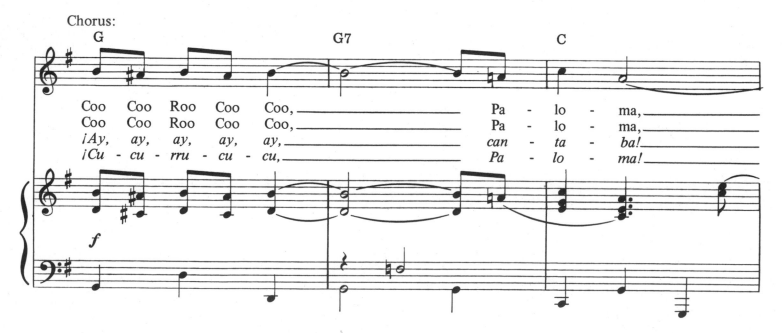

Coo   Coo   Roo   Coo   Coo,_____   Pa - lo - ma,_____
Coo   Coo   Roo   Coo   Coo,_____   Pa - lo - ma,_____
¡Ay,   ay,   ay,   ay,   ay,_____   can - ta - ba!_____
¡Cu - cu - rru - cu - cu,_____   Pa - lo - ma!_____

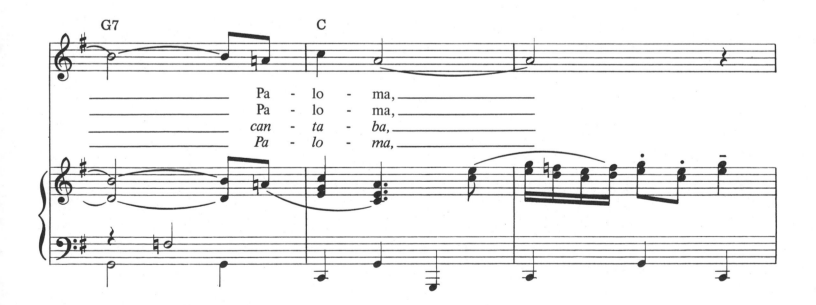

Tell {her/him} that I love _____ {her/him} on - ly! _____
Say my love is true, _____ Pa -
de pa - sión mor - tal, _____ mo - rí - a!
que van a sa - ber _____ de a -

lo - ma! _____
mo - res! _____
Coo Coo Roo Coo Coo! _____
¡Cu - cu - rru - cu - cu! _____

Coo Coo Roo Coo Coo! _____
¡Cu - cu - rru - cu - cu! _____

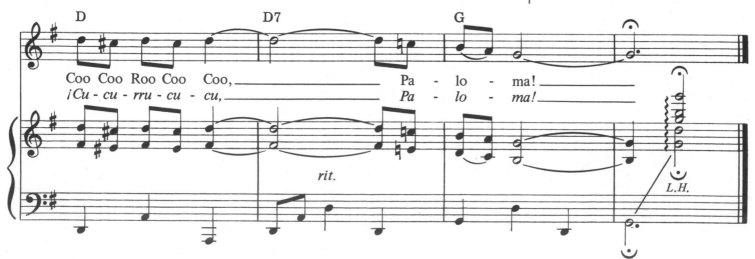

Coo Coo Roo Coo Coo, _____ Pa - lo - ma! _____
¡Cu - cu - rru - cu - cu, _____ Pa - lo - ma! _____

rit.

L.H.

FELIZ NAVIDAD

Lyrics and music by Jose Feliciano

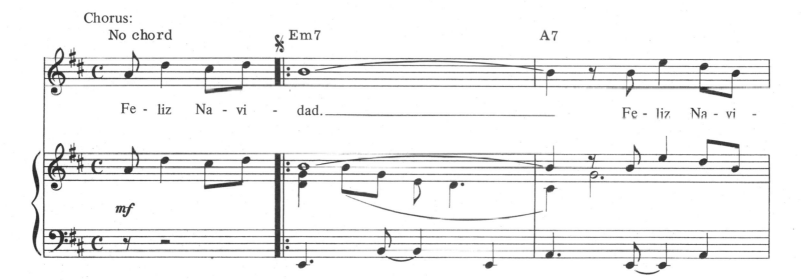

a - ño y fe - li - ci - dad._____ Fe - liz Na - vi -

I want to wish you a _____

Mer - ry Christ-mas, With lots of pres - ents to make you hap - py.

I want to wish you a Mer - ry Christ-mas from the bot - tom of my

THE FOUR WINDS

English lyrics by Jacqueline Sharpe
Spanish lyrics and music by Ernesto Lecuona

Warm as the west wind _____ kiss- ing the flow - ers, _____
Si tu su - pie - ras _____ lo que he pe - na - do _____

That was your laugh - ter___ when our love___ was new.___
des - de a-quel dí - a___ que hu - is - te___ de mí,

Soft as the south wind___ bless - ing the hours,
si tu su - pie - ras lo que he llo - ra - do,

That was your voice say - ing you'd be
lo que he llo - ra - do pen - san - do en

true.___ Chill as the east wind___ bring - ing the
tí.___ Si tu su - pie - ras___ la cruel he -

rain - drops,_____ That was the day when_ you said we must
ri - da _____ *que tu a-ban-do - no_ en mi pe-cho a-*

part._____ Cold as the north wind,_____ That's how you've
brió,_____ y que go - zo - so_____ die - ra la

left me,_____ And all The Four Winds_ have bro-ken my
vi - da _____ por-que llo - ra - ses_ co - mo llo - ro

heart._____ Warm as the heart._____
yo._____ Si tu su - yo._____

FRENESI

English lyrics by Ray Charles and S.K. Russell
Spanish lyrics and music by Alberto Dominguez

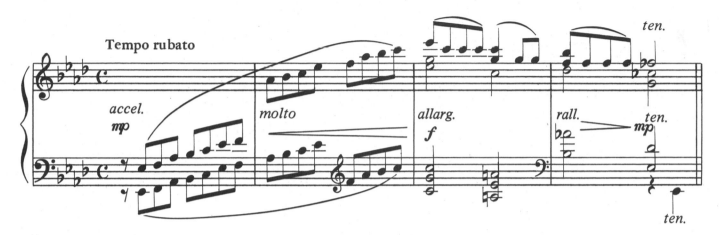

Verse:

Some-time a - go I wan-der'd down in-to old Mex - i - co,___
Bé - sa-me tú a mí, bé - su me i-gual que mi bo - ca te be - só,___

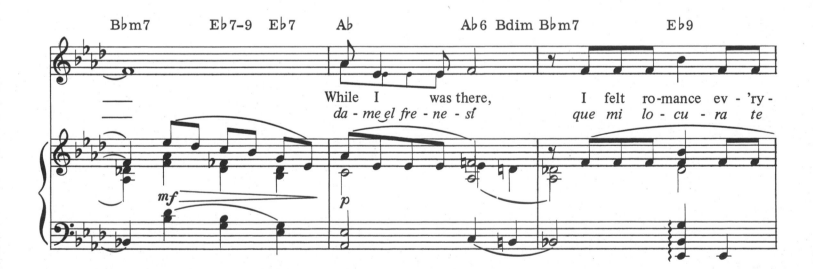

While I was there, I felt ro-mance ev - 'ry
da - me el fre - ne - sí que mi lo - cu - ra te

Full Moon

English lyrics by Bob Russell
Spanish lyrics by Gonzalo Curiel
Music by Gonzalo Curiel and Marcelene Odette

quet; _____ Though you've been ad-
mired for the long-est time, You're
not quite as great as they say. _____

Don't think it's be - cause of your
la lu - na se ve blan - ca,

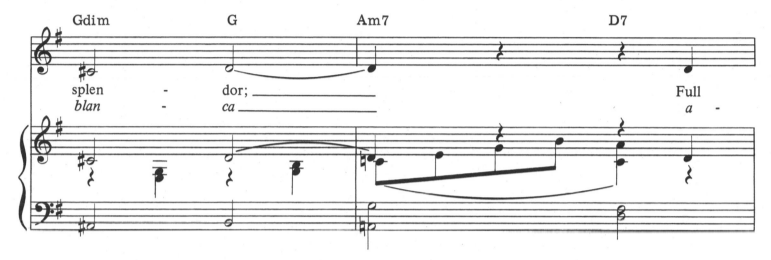

splen - dor; ____ Full
blan - ca ____ *a -*

Moon, ____ I know what ro - mance is,
qui ____ *en ple - no de - rro - che*

E - nough of your sly, know - ing
de lu - na y de mar su - fro,

THE GREATEST PERFORMANCE OF MY LIFE

English lyrics by R.I. Allen
Spanish lyrics and music by Sandro and Oscar Anderle

Moderately slow

Freely, with expression

C7   Fm

Bb11

Bb7

To - night   I gave The Great - est   Per - form - ance Of My
Mas hoy   *que es - toy tan so - lo y tan can - sa - do de llo -*

Eb   C7   Fm

Life;   I nev - er lost con - trol, I played the part so well   that not a
rar   *quie - ro sa - ber si tú que - rrí - as re - gre - sar*   *jun - to a mi*

So
faces, I had to try to make them think that it was true.
vie - jo, A - sí mi al - ma tu_i - ma - gen a - rro - jó.

And
I, who hard - ly dance, danced through the night just like a gyp - sy,_____
sí co - mo se mar - cha la no - che con el dí - a,_____

And
I, who sel - dom drink, drank like a fish till I was high.
sí co - mo se_a - le - ja_un ve - le - ro ha - cia_al - ta mar.

till
I, who had - n't laughed since God knows when, out-laughed Pa - gliac - ci,_____
sí co - mo se_es - ca - pa el a - gua en - tre los de - dos,_____

A -

A -

A -

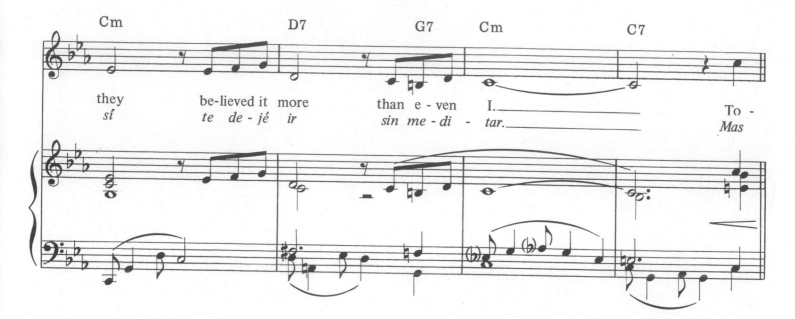

they be-lieved it more than e - ven I._____ To -
sí te de - jé ir sin me - di - tar._____ Mas

night I gave The Great-est Per-form-ance Of My Life; I nev - er
hoy que es-toy tan so - lo y tan can - sa - do de llo - rar quie-ro sa -

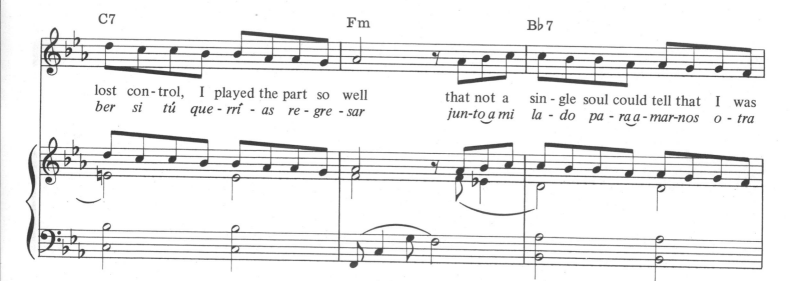

lost con-trol, I played the part so well that not a sin - gle soul could tell that I was
ber si tú que - rrí - as re - gre - sar jun-to a mi la - do pa - ra a - mar-nos o - tra

ly - ing,_____ But love, if you had been be - hind the cur - tain when it
vez._____ Tal vez es - tás pen - san - do que no quie - ra ya de

fell, When all the lights were out and I was all a - lone, you would have
ti e - se ca - lor que al - gu - na vez yo te o - fre - cí y que des -

seen, this { ac - tress / ac - tor } cry - ing._____
pués a - ban - do - né A - sí, A - sí.

For English Lyric | *For Spanish Lyric*

A GAY RANCHERO

English lyrics by Abe Tuvim and Francia Luban
Spanish lyrics and music by J.J. Espinosa

1. A_____ Gay Ran - che - ro, a_____ ca - bal -
2. Back_____ on his ran - cho, we_____ now find
1. *Va - mos a Te - pa* *tie - rra so -*
2. *En_____ el po - tre - ro* *de_____ los mai -*

le - ro Can_____ al - ways find some - one to
Pan - cho With_____ his Pe - pi - ta by his
ña - da *don - de la vi - da_es* *un pri -*
za - les *ten - go_un pe - da - zo* *de jar -*

pet._____ A_____ se - ño - ri - ta,
side._____ She_____ thinks he's hand - some,
mor,_____ *a - llá me_es - pe - ra*
dín,_____ *co - mo lo rie - go*

a ____ sweet Pe - pi - ta
worth __ an - y ran - som,
mi__ cha - pe - tea - da
to - das las tar - des

Her____ oth - er
To____ him she's
la ú - ni - ca
ya__ dió bo -

C

loves will soon for - get._____
still the blush - ing bride._____
due - ña de mi a - mor._____
to - nes el jaz - mín._____

If____ he's in -
Our____ Gay Ran -
Es__ tan bo -
A - sí le

sis - tent
che - ro,
ni - ta
pa - sa a

and____ she's not dis - tant,
our____ ca - bal - le - ro
mi____ cha - pa - rri - ta
mi____ vir - gen - ci - ta

The____ se - ño -
Still____ tells the
que__ cuan - do
cuan - do le

ri - ta will con - fess_____ Her Gay Ran -
world of how they met._____ This Gay Ran -
vá al tem - plo a re - zar,_____ to - dos le
doy to - do mi a - mor,_____ ya le a na -

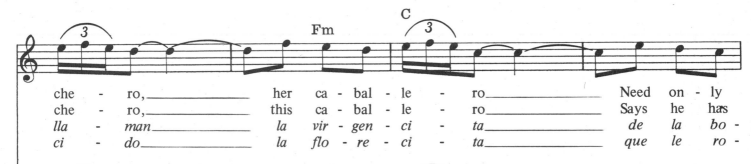

che - ro,_____ her ca - bal - le - ro_____ Need on - ly
che - ro,_____ this ca - bal - le - ro_____ Says he has
lla - man_____ la vir - gen - ci - ta_____ de la bo -
ci - do_____ la flo - re - ci - ta_____ que le ro -

ask and she'll say yes._____
noth - ing to re - gret._____
qui - ta de co - ral. } *Que*
bé del co - ra - zón. }

Soon there'll be a fies - ta with a blush - ing
Now to end the sto - ry that I once was
lin - das las ma - ña - nas cuan - do sa - le el

bride,
told,
sol   a - -

And A Gay Ran - che - ro stand - ing
Here's a lit - tle se - cret that I
sí son las Al - te - ñas de es - te al -

gliss.

by her side.
must un - fold:
re - de - dor.   A - -

If they find the
For they found the
le - gres y bo -

gliss.

prom - ise that they have in store,
prom - ise that they had in store,
ni - tas to - do_el tiem - po_es - tán las

They'll be count - ing lit - tle chic - os by the
Now they're real - ly count - ing chic - os by the
lin - das Al - te - ñi - tas de Te - pa - tit -

score.
lán.

score.
lán.

GRANADA

English lyrics by Dorothy Dodd
Music by Augustin Lara

Verse:

Gra - na - da, _____ I'm fall - ing un-der your spell, _____ And if you could speak, what a fas - ci - nat-ing tale you would tell, _____ Of an

age ___ the world has long for - got - ten, ___ of an age ___ that weaves a

si - lent mag - ic in Gra - na - da to - day. ___

The dawn in the sky greets the day with a
when day is done and the sun starts a to

sigh for Gra - na - da. ___
set in Gra - na - da.

Dm7 G7

For she can re-
I en - vy the

G9   G7   Dm7   G7

mem - ber   the   splen - dor   that   once   was   Gra -
blush of   the   snow - clad   Si - er - ra   Ne -

C   C6   *To Coda* ⊕

na - da.
va - da.

                 C   C6

It   still   can   be   found   in   the

hills all a - round as I wan - der a - long,

En -

tranc'd by the beau - ty be - fore me, En -

tranc'd by a land full of sun - shine and

Green Eyes

English lyrics by L. Wolfe Gilbert
Spanish lyrics by Adolfo Utrera
Music by Nilo Menendez

Tempo Bolero

Moderately, with expression

Verse:

You have such change-a-ble eyes, they haunt me.

Fue - ron tus o - jos los que me die - ron

To some, they're brown and to oth-ers blue._____
*El te-ma dul-ce de mi can-ción.*_____

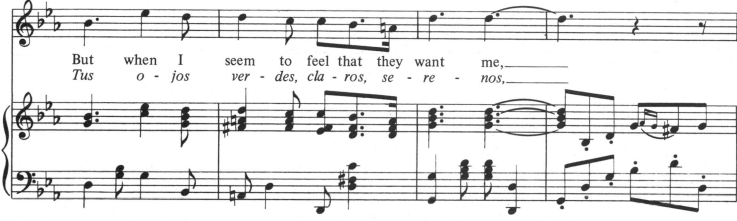

But when I seem to feel that they want me,_____
*Tus o-jos ver-des, cla-ros, se-re-nos,*_____

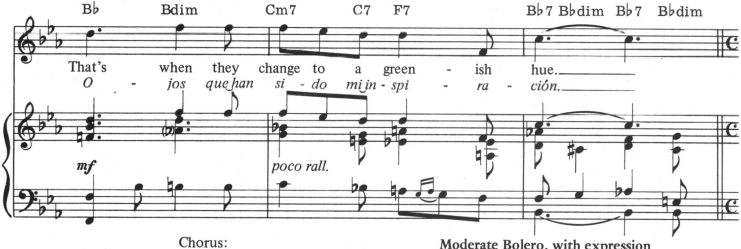

That's when they change to a green-ish hue._____
*O - jos que han si-do mi in-spi-ra-ción.*_____

mf *poco rall.*

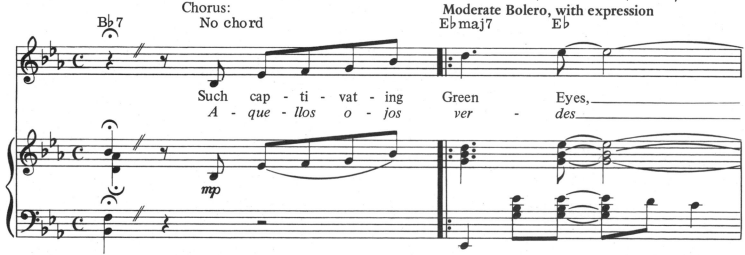

Chorus:
No chord

Moderate Bolero, with expression

Such cap-ti-vat-ing Green Eyes,_____
*A-que-llos o-jos ver - des*_____

mp

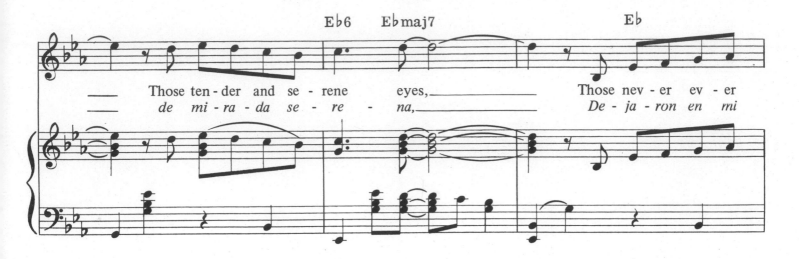

Those ten-der and se-rene eyes,_____ Those nev-er ev-er
de mi-ra-da se-re-na,_____ De-ja-ron en mi

mean eyes,_____ They're so lov-ing and true._____
al - ma_____ E-ter-na sed de_a - mar._____

_____ The sea be-neath the blue skies_____ Is re-flect-ing your
An-he-los de ca-ri - cias_____ De be-sos y ter-

Green Eyes,_____ And the trees in the wood - land_____
nu - ras,_____ De to-das las dul - zu - ras_____

132

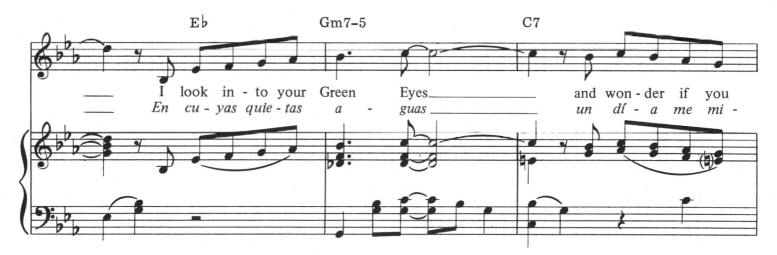

And when-ev - er I doubt you,_____ I look in - to your
Que en mi al-ma han de - ja - do,_____ A - que - llos o - jos

Green Eyes_____ and I find my heav - en there._____
ver - des_____ que yo nun - ca be - sa - ré._____

Such cap - ti - vat - ing there._____
A - que - llos o - jos ré._____

GUADALAJARA

Spanish lyrics and music by Pepe Guizar

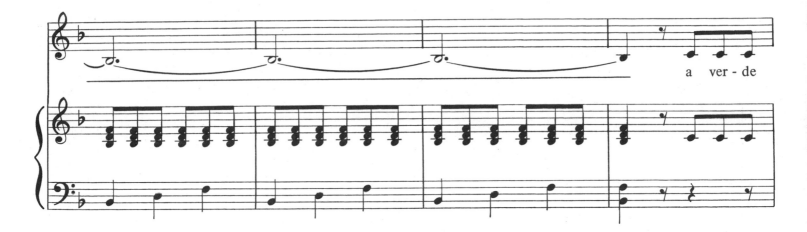

a ver - de

ja - ra fres - ca del ri - o, son mil pa - lo - mos tu ca - se - rí - o, Gua - da - la -

ja - ra, Gua - da - la - ja - ra sa - bes a pu - ra tie - rra mo - ja - da.

D.C. al Coda 1

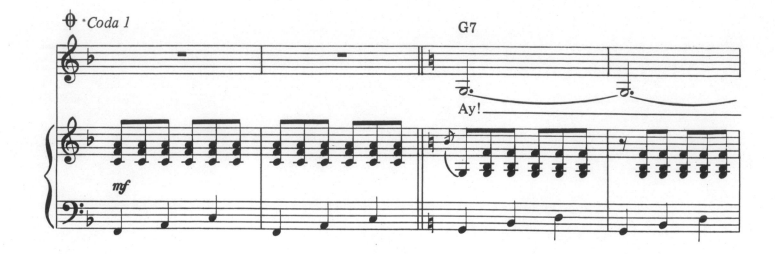

da - bles co - mo las tar - des en que la llu - via des - de la lo - ma ir - nos ha -

ci - a has - ta Za - po - pam. _____

D.C. al Coda 2

Coda 2

Gua - da - la - ja - ra! _____

Freely

____ Gua - da - la - ja - ra! _____

It Doesn't Matter

Lyrics and music by Jose Feliciano

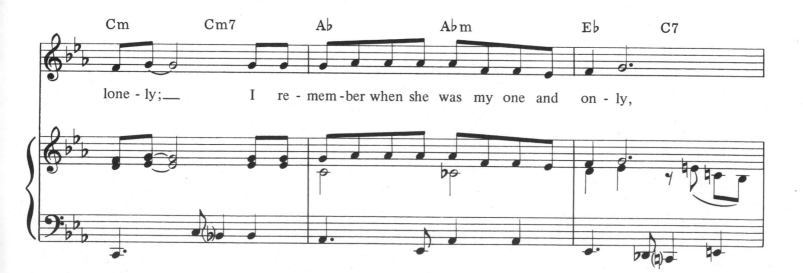

But I guess It Does-n't Mat-ter an-y-way.

When I think of___ all the times I made her cry, I hope she

knows by now___ that I was just a lit-tle high and I am

sor-ry,___ But I guess It Does-n't Mat-ter an-y-

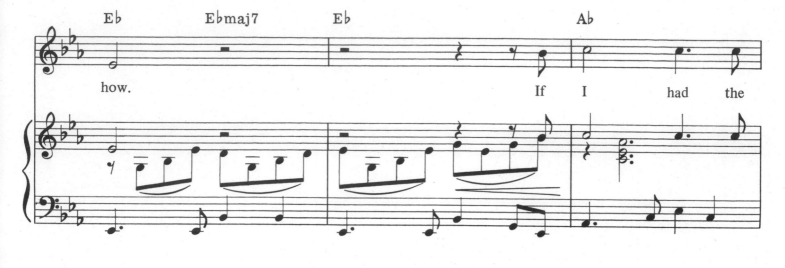

how.   If I had the

time   I would try and___   find my mind,   The

years have quick-ly gone by,   and there's no   time___   for a lone - ly

guy.___   But   if you   see her,___   tell her that I real - ly care and that I

IT'S IMPOSSIBLE

Lyrics by Sid Wayne
Music by A. Manzanero

Slowly, with expression

It's Im - pos-si - ble,   Tell the   sun to leave the sky, It's just im - pos-si - ble,

It's Im - pos-si - ble,   Ask a   ba - by not to cry, It's just im -

pos - si - ble. Can I hold you__ clos-er to me,__ and not

feel you__ go - ing through me,__ Split the sec - ond__ that I

nev - er think of you? Oh, how im - pos - si - ble. Can the

o - cean__ keep from rush-ing to the shore? It's just im - pos-si - ble. If I

had you,__ could I ev - er want for more? It's just im - pos-si - ble.

And to - mor-row,__ should you ask me for the world,some-how I'd get it,__ I would

sell my ver - y soul and not re - gret it,____ For to live with-out your love is just im -

pos - si - ble. It's Im - pos - si - ble. Im -

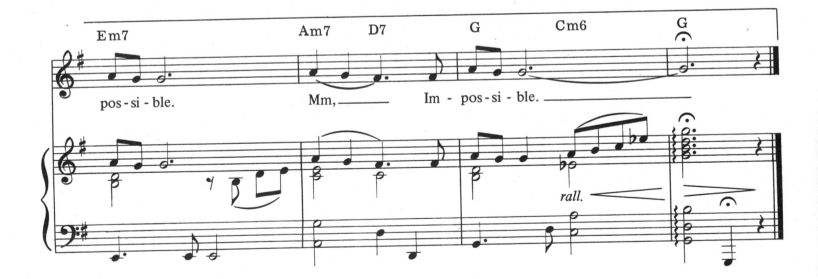

pos - si - ble. Mm,____ Im - pos - si - ble.____

LISBON ANTIGUA

English lyrics by Harry Dupree
Music by Raul Portela, J. Galhardo and A. do Vale

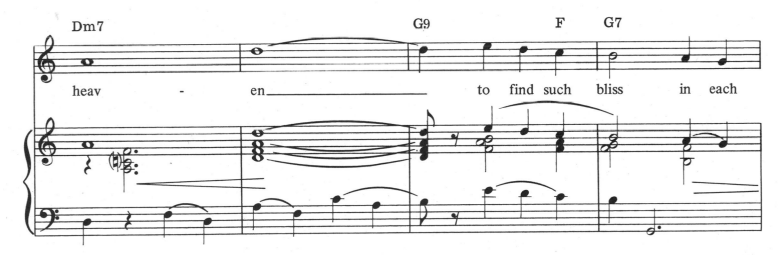

Verse:

Por - tu - gal,_____ Lis - bon was gay in the moon - light,_____ The stars were shin - ing a - bove_____ when I found you,_____ my_____

love._____ What is this

strange - ness, this splen - dor, all this

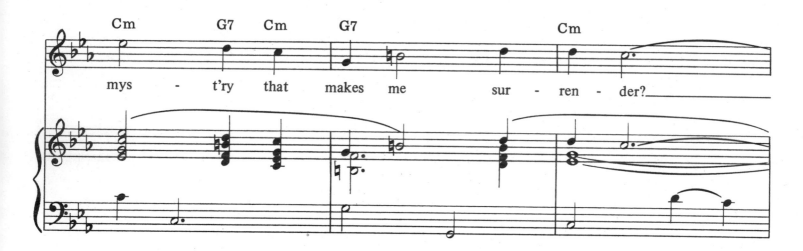

mys - t'ry that makes me sur - ren - der?_____

I gave my

152

LOVE ME WITH ALL YOUR HEART

English lyrics by Sunny Skylar
Spanish lyrics by Mario Rigual
Music by Carlos Rigual

Moderately slow, with a beat

Love Me With All Your Heart,— That's all I want, love;—
Cuan-do ca-lien-ta el sol— a-qui en la pla-ya

Love me with all of your heart or not at all;—
sien-to tu cuer-po vi-brar cer-ca de mí,—

Just prom-ise me this:___ that you'll give me___ all your kiss-es,___ Ev-'ry
Es tu pal-pi-tar,___ es tu ca-ra,___ es tu pe-lo,___ son tus

poco a poco cresc.

win - ter,___ ev-'ry sum - mer,___ ev-'ry fall;
be - sos,___ me es-tre-mez-co___ o - o - o;

When we are far a-part___ or when you're near me,___
Cuan-do ca-lien-ta el sol___ a-quí en la pla-ya,___

Love me with all of your heart as I love you;___
sien-to tu cuer-po vi-brar cer-ca de mí,___

MAGIC IS THE MOONLIGHT

English lyrics by Charles Pasquale
Spanish lyrics and music by Maria Grever

Moderately slow

Verse:

Te quie - ro,_____ sweet heav - en,_____
Te quie - ro,_____ di - jis - te,_____

Here un - der your spell I am caught in a whirl - pool of
To - man - do mis ma - nos en - tre tus ma - ni - tas de

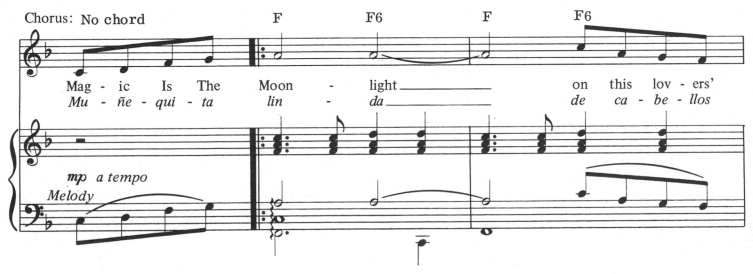

MALAGUEÑA

English lyrics by Marian Banks
Spanish lyrics and music by Ernesto Lecuona

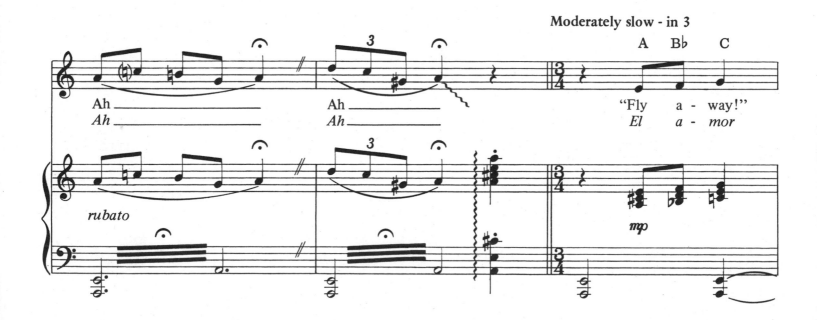

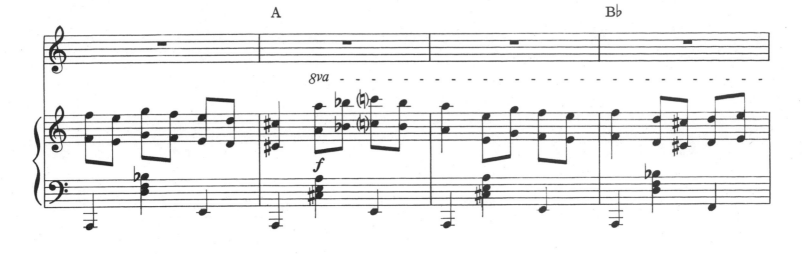

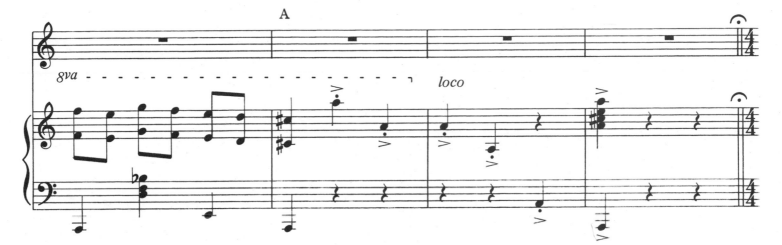

Flamenco tempo - in 4

My Ma - la - gue - ña, your eyes shamed the pur-ple sky.

Ma - la - gue - ña de o - jos ne - gros

You were as fair as I dreamed you would be;_____
*Ma - la - gue - ña de mis sue - ños.*_____

I loved and left you, for I nev - er could de - ny The
Me es - toy mu - rien - do de pe - - na por

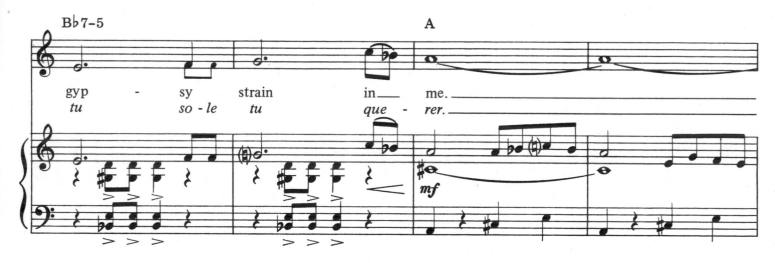

gyp - sy strain in__ me._____
*tu so - le tu que - rer.*_____

_____
_____ Light - ly as a song, go - ing where I
La la la la la la la la la la

please; Jour-ney-ing a - long with ev - 'ry va - grant breeze. Up a
la   la la la la   la la la la la la la la   Ma - la-gue -

hill,   down a   stream, I   fol - low in   a   dream.
ña   re - bo - ni - ta   te   quie - ro   be - sar.

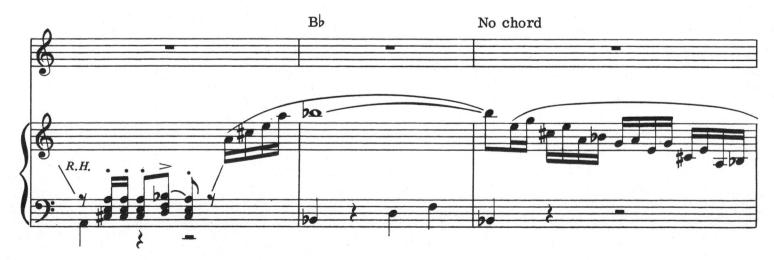

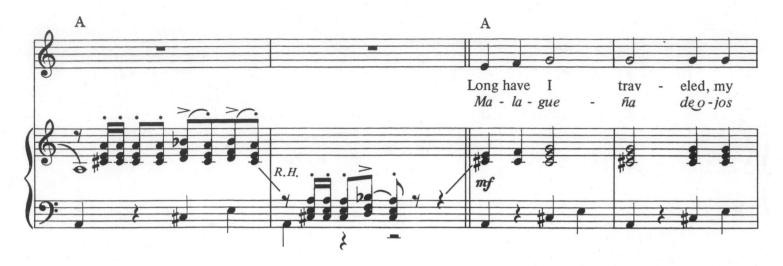

Long have I trav - eled, my
Ma - la - gue - ña de o - jos

love, since the night we met._____ Seek - ing in wan-d'ring a
ne - gros_____ Ma - la - gue - ña de mis

way to for - get._____ But it's no mat - ter by
sue - ños._____ me es - toy mu - rien - do de

what path I may de - part, I can't es - cape from my
pe - na, por tu so - le tu que -

Maria Elena

English lyrics by S.K. Russell
Spanish lyrics and music by Lorenzo Barcelata

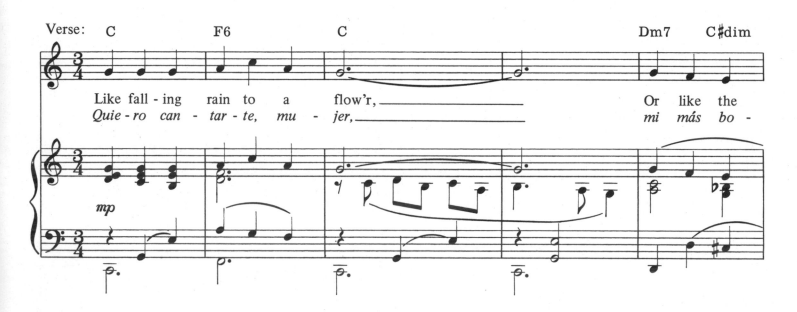

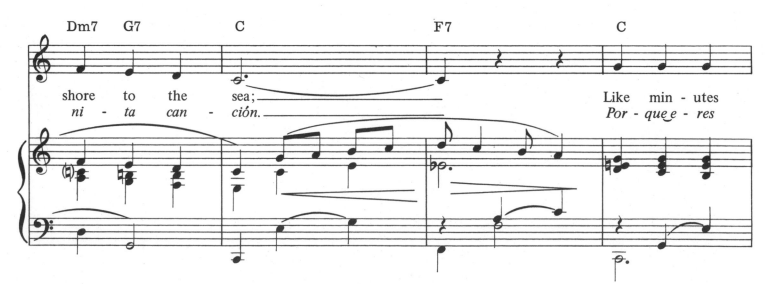

are to an hour,_____ Dar-ling, so you are to
tú mi que - rer,_____ *rei - na de mi co - ra -*

me._____ This I can nev-er dis-
zón._____ *No me_a - ban - do - nes, mi*

guise,_____ Here in my heart or my eyes._____
bien,_____ *que_e-res to - do mi que - rer._____*

Chorus:

Ma-ri-a_E - le - na, you're the an - swer to a pray'r,_____
¡Tu-yo_es mi co - ra - zón, oh, sol de mi que - rer,_____

mp-mf

Ma - ri - a E - le - na, can't you see how much I care?
mu - jer de mi i - lu - sión, mi a - mor te con - sa - gré!

To me your voice is like the ech - o of a
Mi vi - da la em - be - lle - ce u - na es - pe - ran - za a -

sigh, And when you're near, my heart can't speak a - bove a
zul, mi vi - da tie - ne un cie - lo que le dis - te

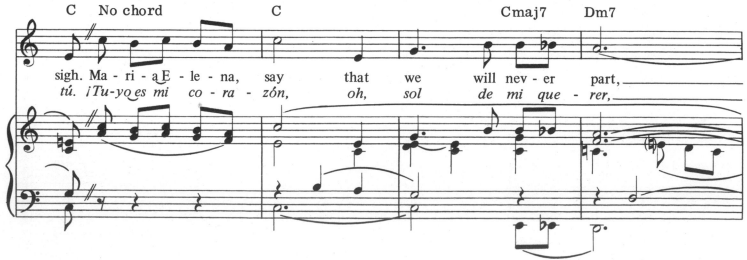

sigh. Ma - ri - a E - le - na, say that we will nev - er part, ____
tú. ¡Tu - yo es mi co - ra - zón, oh, sol de mi que - rer,

Ma - ri - a E - le - na, take me to your heart;
tu - yo es to - do mi ser, tu - yo es, mu - jer!

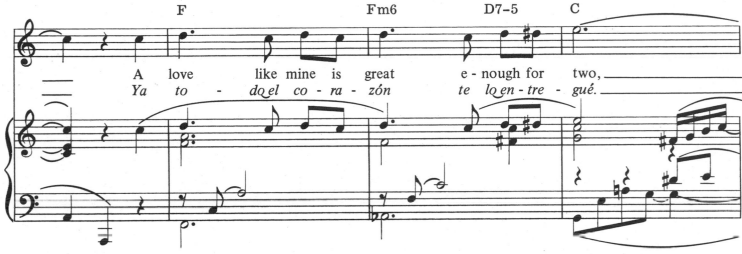

A love like mine is great e - nough for two,
Ya to - do el co - ra - zón te lo en - tre - gué.

To share this love is real - ly all I ask of you.
¡E - res mi fe, e - res mi Dios, e - res mi a - mor!

Ma - ri - a E - le - na, you, my love.
Tu - yo es mi co - ra - mor, mi a - mor!

MAS QUE NADA

English lyrics by Loryn Deane
Portuguese lyrics and music by Jorge Ben

me _____ 'til I feel like I'm gon - na ex - plode. _____ Oh, this is
-sar, _____ Pois o sam - ba es - tá a - ni - ma - do, O que

what you do _____ to me! _____ Are _____ your lips _____
eu que - ro e sam - bar. _____ Es - se sam -

say - ing things _____ that you feel in your heart? _____
ba _____ Que é mix - to de ma - ra - ca - tú _____

If your heart is beat - ing mad - ly, _____ Then _____
E sam - ba de pre - to vel - lho, _____ Sam -

MIAMI BEACH RUMBA

English lyrics by Albert Gamse
Spanish lyrics by Johnnie Camacho
Music by Irving Fields

Moderately

I start-ed out to go to Hai - ti,
De pa - so en mi via - je a Cu - ba,

Soon I was at Mi - am - i

Beach.
ré;

There, not so ver - y far from Hai - ti,
Ya - sí cer - qui - ta de mi Cu - ba,

Quaint are the danc - es they teach!
Rum - bean-do a - llí me que - dé.

That's where the or - ang - es are
La chi - ca que me pre - sen -

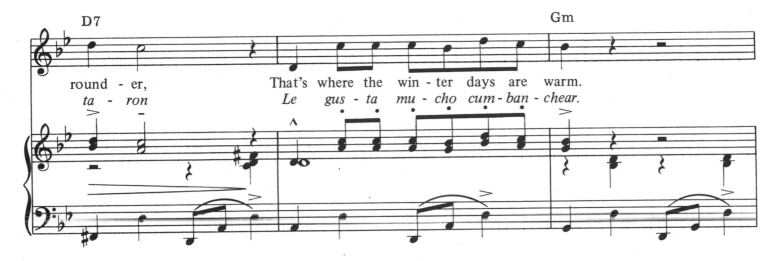

round - er,
ta - ron

That's where the win - ter days are warm.
Le gus - ta mu - cho cum - ban - chear.

That's where I caught a hun - dred pound - er,
Por e - so no voy más a Cu - ba,

We danced in true Lat - in
Si es que yo quie - ro rum -

form.
bear.

Here was all the charm of Hai - ti,
To - dos di - rán que ma - ña - na,

The
De

tropic sky was just as fair, The temp'rature was over
éste lugar yo me iré; En cambio yo sé que ma-

eighty, Which they call 'cool' down there!
ñana, Con ella estaré.

I did-n't go where I in-tend-ed, Far great-er joy was in my
Y cuando por fin nos ca-se-mos, Es cier-to que en Mi-a-mi

reach, My Car-ib-be-an cruise was end-ed In a
Beach, La luna de miel pa-sa-re-mos, Con la

MISIRLOU

English lyrics by Fred Wise, Milton Leeds and S.K. Russell
Spanish lyrics by J. Pina
Music by N. Roubanis

Moderate Beguine tempo

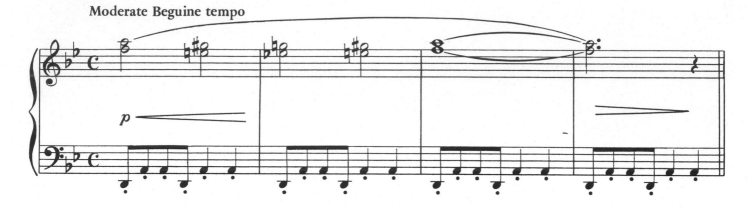

Verse:

Des - ert shad - ows creep a - cross pur - ple sands,_____
Cuan - do a - le - gre tú son - ri - es mu - jer,_____

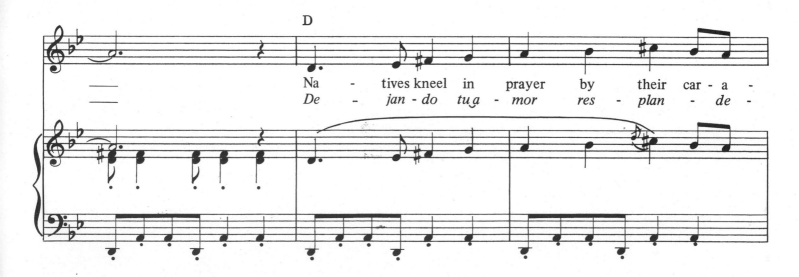

_____ Na - tives kneel in prayer by their car - a -
_____ De - jan - do tu a - mor res - plan - de -

Are the moon and the sun, Fair-est
Del o - rien - te la flor e - res

one. Old Tem-ple Bells are
tú. *Tu mi - rar es des -*

call - ing a - cross the sand,
te - llo de_in - spi - ra - ción,

We'll find our Kis - met an - swer - ing love's com - mand
Que de - ja_em - be - le - sa - do mi ço - ra - zón

182

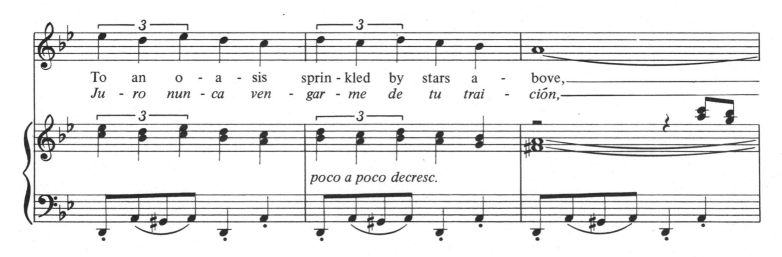

Heav - en will guide us, Al - lah will bless our
Aun - que vi - va en el mun - do sin co - ra -

Gm .... Gm

love. _____ Ah, _____ Ah, _____
zón. _____ Ah, _____ Ah, _____

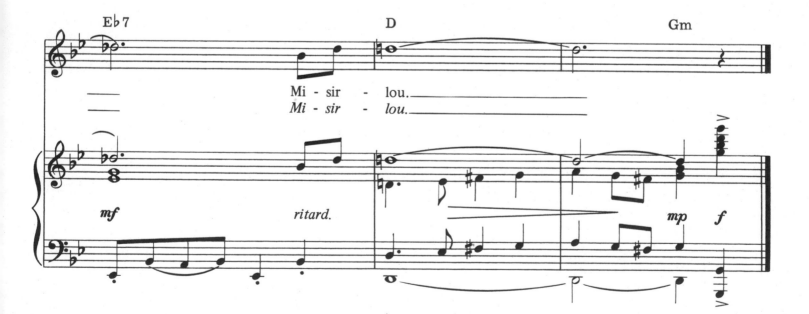

E♭7 .... D .... Gm

Mi - sir - lou. _____
Mi - sir - lou. _____

MI VIDA

English lyrics by Harry Ruby
Spanish lyrics and music by Ernesto Lecuona

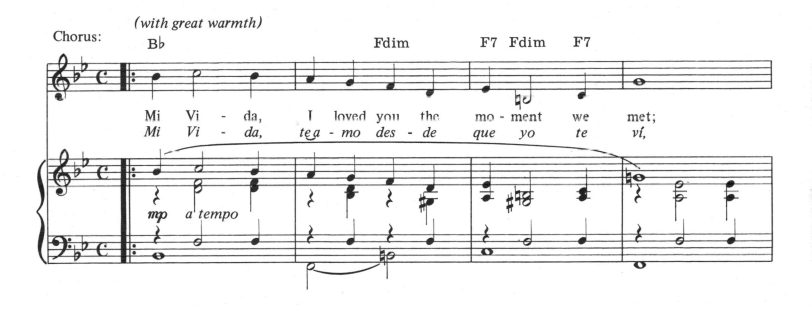

Mi Vi - da, I loved you the mo - ment we met;
Mi Vi - da, te a - mo des - de que yo te ví,

Mi Vi - da, Dreams came true the mo - ment we met.
Mi Vi - da, tu e - res la i - lu - sión pa - ra mí

F7

In some mag - ic way, you came from a -
Co - mo un sue - ño a - zul vi - nis - te fu -

F11   F+5

far, You are here to - day, will
gaz, Den - tro de mi ser yo

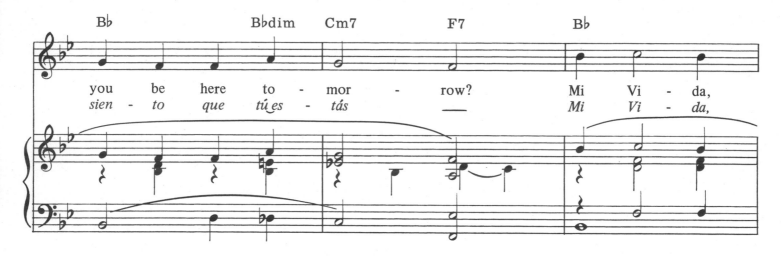

Bb   Bbdim Cm7   F7   Bb

you be here to - mor - row? Mi Vi - da,
sien - to que tú es - tás Mi Vi - da,

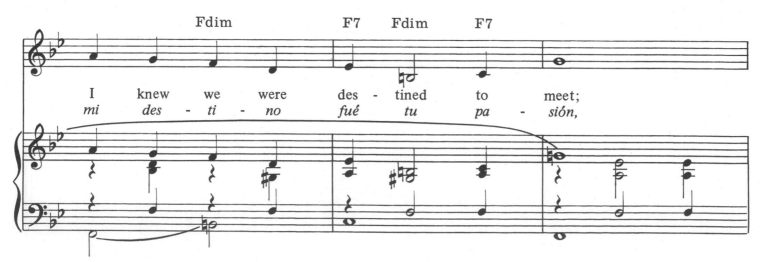

Fdim   F7 Fdim   F7

I knew we were des - tined to meet;
mi des - ti - no fué tu pa - sión,

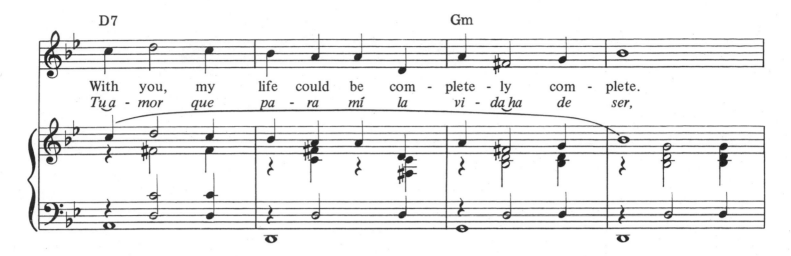

With you, my life could be com - plete - ly com - plete.
Tu a - mor que pa - ra mí la vi - da ha de ser,

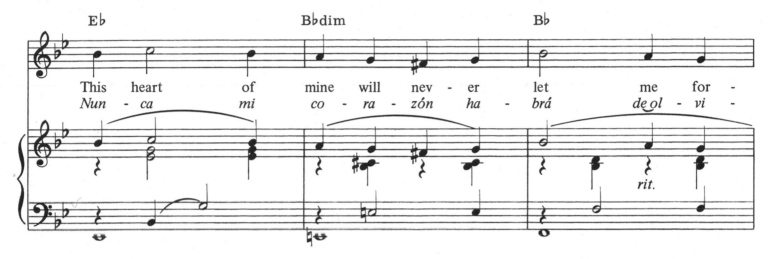

This heart of mine will nev - er let me for -
Nun - ca mi co - ra - zón ha - brá de ol - vi -

get. You and the mo - ment we
dar. A - que - lla vez que te

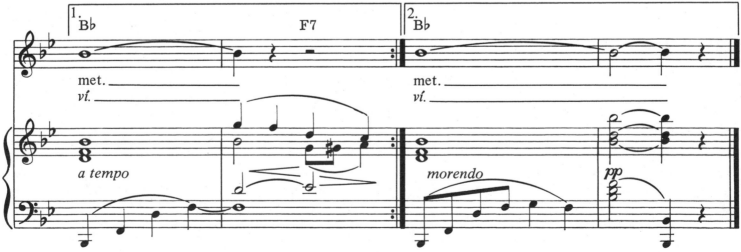

met. _____
ví. _____
a tempo

met. _____
ví. _____
morendo   *pp*

MY ADOBE HACIENDA

Lyrics and music by Louise Massey and Lee Penny

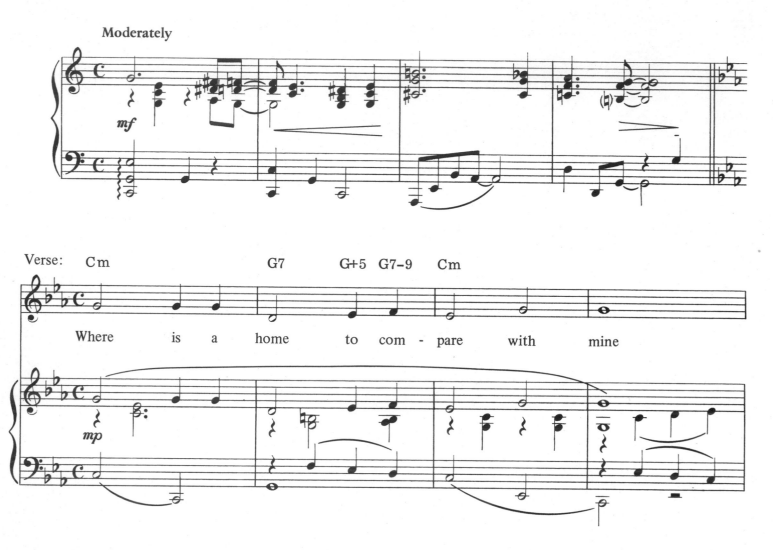

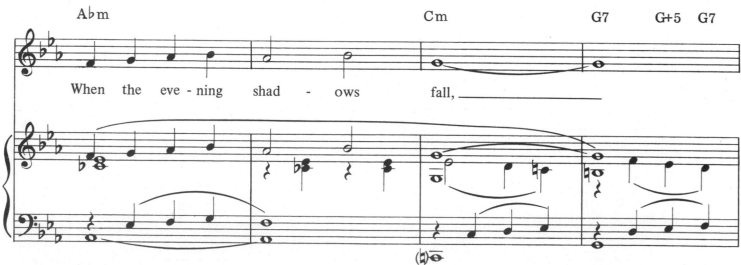

MY RIVAL

English lyrics by Abe Tuvim
Spanish lyrics and music by Maria Teresa Lara

Moderately, not too slow

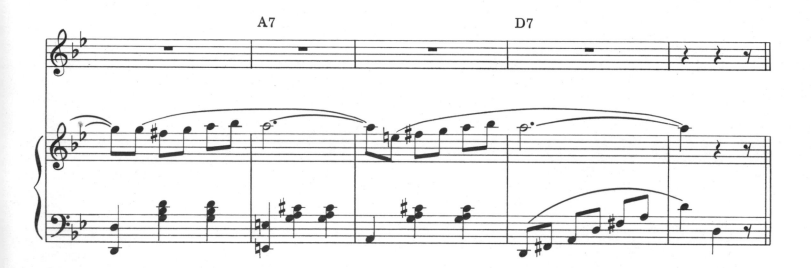

Verse:

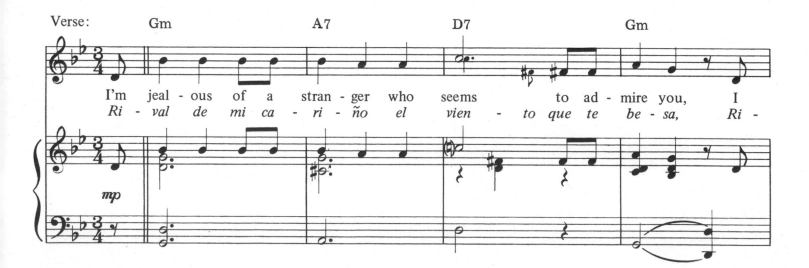

I'm jeal - ous of a stran - ger who seems to ad - mire you, I
Ri - val de mi ca - ri - ño el vien - to que te be - sa, Ri -

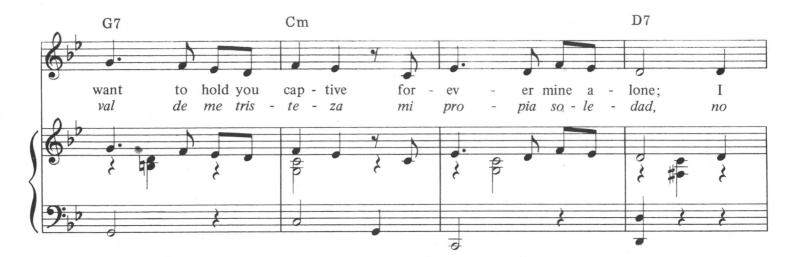

want to hold you cap - tive for - ev - er mine a - lone; I
val de me tris - te - za mi pro - pia so - le - dad, no

al - ways feel a dan - ger when some - one de - sires you, I
quie - ro que te va - yas, no quie - ro que me de - jes, me

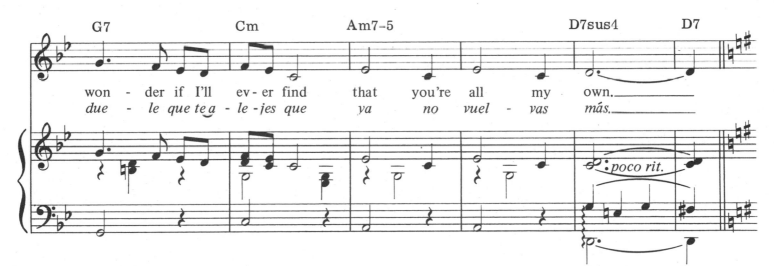

won - der if I'll ev - er find that you're all my own._____
due - le que te a - le - jes que ya no vuel - vas más._____

Chorus:

For the sun - shine that kiss - es your beau - ti - ful lips is My
Mi Ri - val es mi pro - pio co - ra - zón por trai - cio -

Ri - val_____ And I en - vy each
ne - ro,_____ yo no sé co - mo

flow - er you hold in your del - i - cate hands, dear._____
pue - do a - bo - rre - cer - te si tan - to te quie - ro,_____

_____ When you touch me my heart al - most ceas - es to
_____ no me ex - pli - co por - qué me a - tor - men - ta el ren -

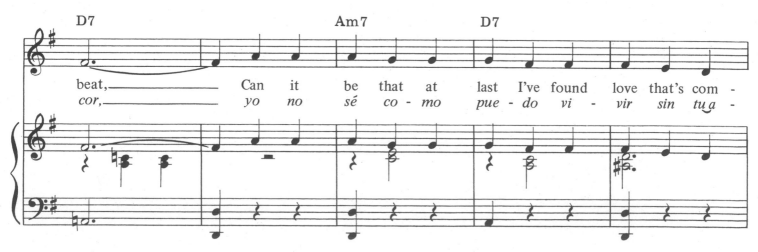

beat,_____ Can it be that at last I've found love that's com -
cor,_____ yo no sé co - mo pue - do vi - vir sin tu a -

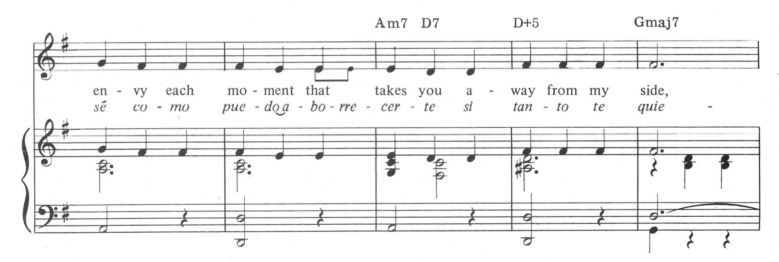

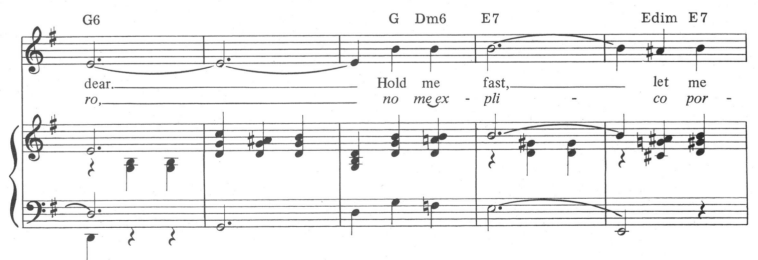

MY SHAWL

English lyrics by Stanley Adams
Spanish lyrics by Pedro Berrios
Music by Xavier Cugat

Moderately slow

Verse:

In some Cu - ban town _____ you
A llá en el ba - tey, _____ A

stop watch - ing an old mak - er of shawls, _____
llá ba - jo la som - bra de un pal - mar, _____

dreams   for ev -'ry   maid, _____ A
ca - do y sin ce - sar, _____ *Lle -*

shawl   in his   hand, _____ His
nos   de e - mo - ción, _____ *El*

call   reach - es their hearts   as they pa - rade. _____
om - bo   re - pi - ca - ba sin ce - sar. _____

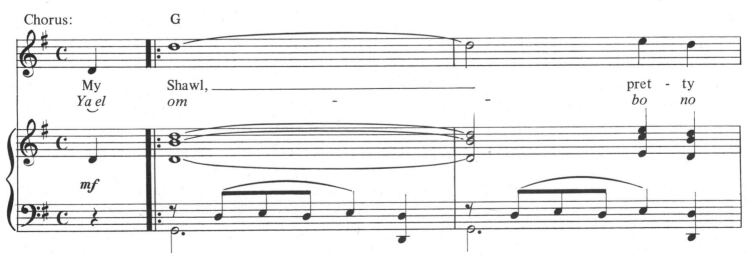

Chorus:

My   Shawl, _____ pret - ty
Ya el   om — — — — *bo   no*

la - dy,_____ try it on you._____
can - ta,_____ ya se ol - vi - dó.

Buy My Shawl_____ spun in
Su rit - - mo sal -

mag - ic,_____ wish - es come true._____
va - je_____ se ter - mi - nó.

Its glo - ry_____ weaves a
Tan so - lo_____ ya se

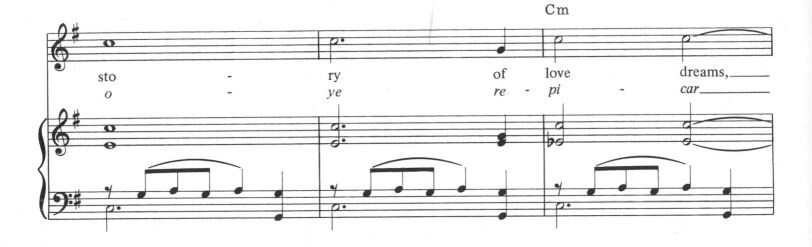

sto - ry of love dreams,_____
o - ye re - pi - car_____

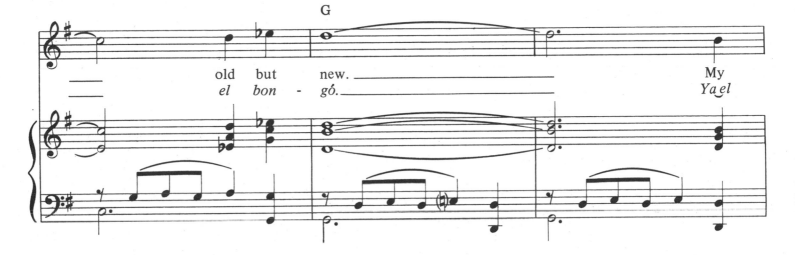

_____ old but new._____ My
el bon - gó._____ Ya el

Shawl _____ brings a ro - mance,_____
om - - bo no can ta _____

_____ may - be for you._____ My
_____ ya en - mu - de - ció._____ Ya el

Noche Azul

English lyrics by Carol Raven
Spanish lyrics and music by Ernesto Lecuona

Moderately slow, with expression

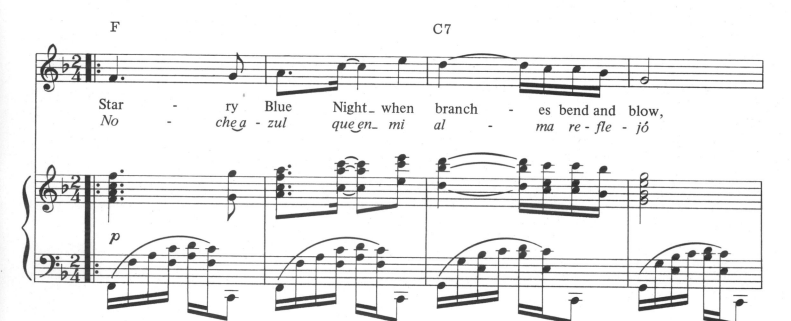

Star - ry Blue Night_ when branch - es bend and blow,
No - che a - zul que en_ mi al - ma re - fle - jó

Love - ly blue night while fan - cies come and go,
la pa - sión que so - ña - ba a - ca - ri - ciar

As_____ in a mir - ror__ re - flect - ed there__ I can
vuel - ve de nue - vo a_ dar paz a mi__ co - ra -

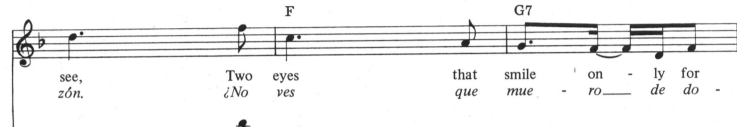

see, Two eyes that smile ' on - ly for
zón. ¿No ves que mue - ro_ de do -

me._____ — Oh,__ come blue
lor?_____ — Ven__ no - cheạ -

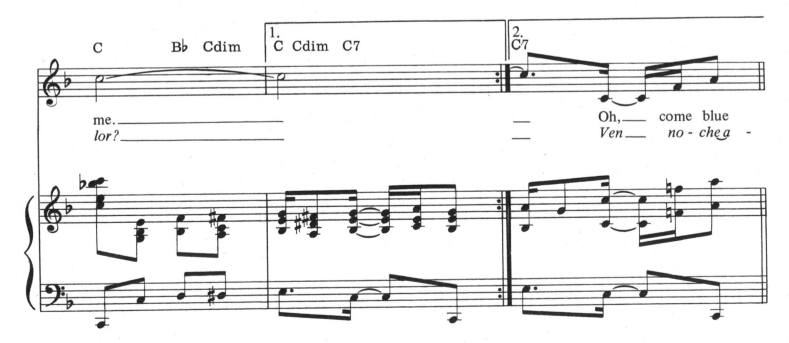

night,_____ and with the light_____ of dreams dis - pel my pain,_____
zul_____ ven o - tra vez_____ a que me des tu luz_____

_____ Where_ sea-winds blow_____ on shores I know,_____ Bring me my
mi - ra que_es - tá_____ mi co - ra - zón_____ an - sio - so

love a - gain,_____ One_ ten - der sign_____ that love is
de a - mar_____ ven o - tra - vez_____ que yo sin

NEGRA CONSENTIDA

English lyrics by Marjorie Harper
Spanish lyrics and music by Joaquin Pardave

Moderately

Verse:

Night - - time,　　　　night -
No - che,　　　　　　no -

time, _____　love's mes-sage I bring. ____
che, _____　te lla-ma el a - mor. ____

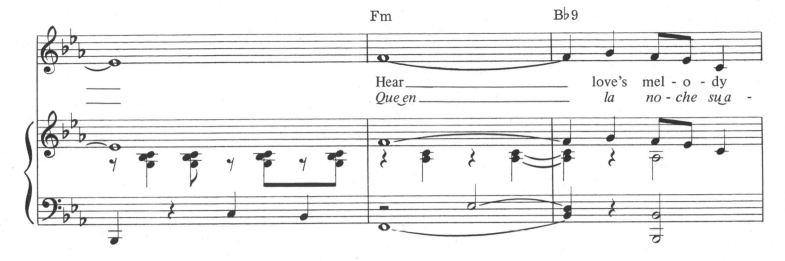

Hear_____ love's mel - o - dy
Que_en_____ la no - che su a -

ring!_____
mor,_____

Hear_____
Te_____

the trou - ba - dour sing!_____
can - ta_el tro - va - dor._____

Chorus:

Love me,_____ My Pet_ Bru - nette, Love me,_____
Ne - gra,_____ ne - gra_ de mi vi - da,_____

And al - ways think of me, _____ As I___ think of
Ne - gra__ con - sen - ti - da, _____ *Quién te__ quie-re a*

you. _____ Hear me, _____
ti? _____ *Mi - ra,* ____

my lit - tle one, cheer me, _____ I need_ you right
mi al - ma__ do - lo - ri - da, _____ *Ne - gra__ de mi*

near me, _____ I want_ you, I do. _____
vi - da, _____ *Y so - lo por ti.* ____

Take me,_____ My Pet_____ Bru-nette,
Ne - gra,_____ ne-gra_____ de mi

take me,_____ How can_____ you for - sake me,_____
vi - da,_____ Ne - gra_____ con - sen - ti - da,_____

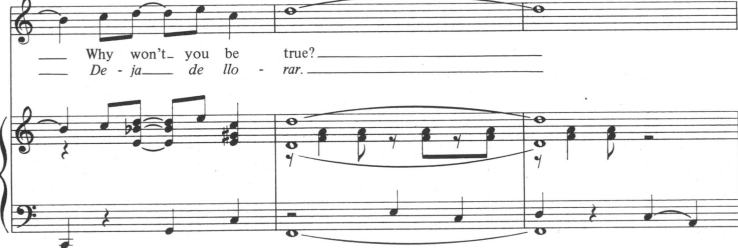

_____ Why won't_____ you be true?_____
_____ *De - ja_____ de llo - rar.*_____

PERFIDIA

English lyrics by Milton Leeds
Spanish lyrics and music by Alberto Dominguez

Stran-gers, and we were sweet-hearts for so long,___
Na - die com - pren - de lo que su - fro yo,___

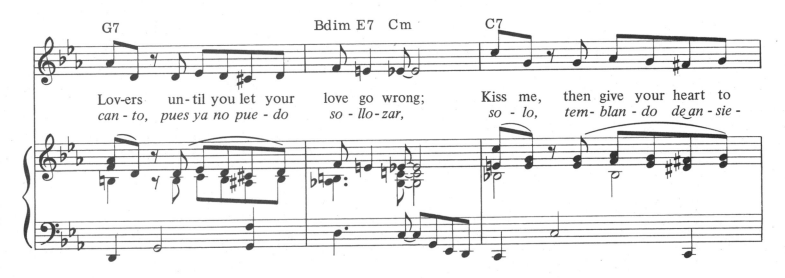

Lov-ers un-til you let your love go wrong;
can - to, pues ya no pue - do so - llo-zar,
Kiss me, then give your heart to
so - lo, tem - blan - do de an - sie-

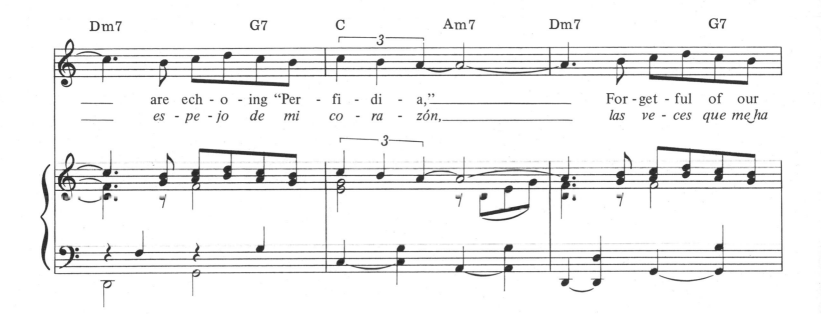

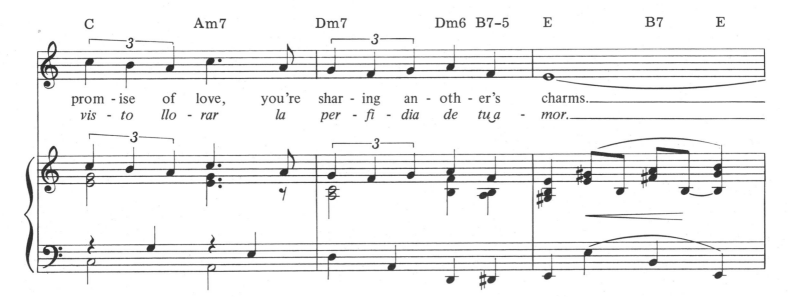

now_____ I know my love was not for you,_____
tú._____ ¡Quién sa - be por don - de an - da - rás,_____

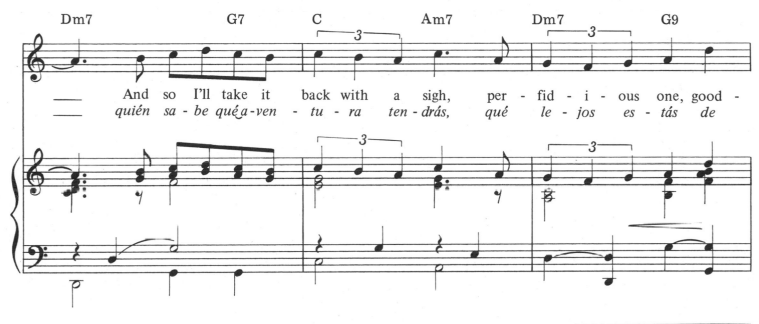

_____ And so I'll take it back with a sigh, per - fid - i - ous one, good -
_____ quién sa - be qué a - ven - tu - ra ten - drás, qué le - jos es - tás de

bye._____
mí!_____

To bye._____
Mu - mí!_____

PATRICIA, IT'S PATRICIA

Lyrics by Bob Marcus
Music by Perez Prado

Moderately

Chorus:

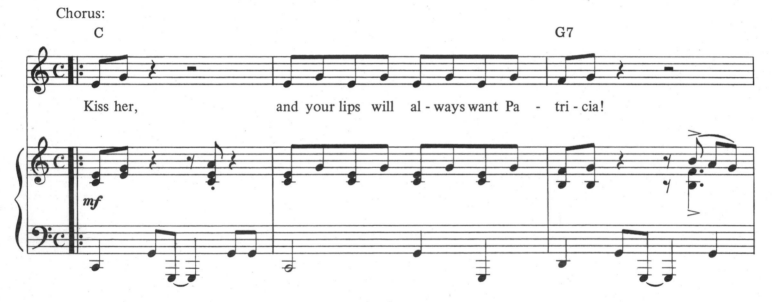

Kiss her, and your lips will al - ways want Pa - tri - cia!

Stroll her, see Pa - tri - cia move with all her

charms! _____ Mam-bo, cha-cha or me-ren-gue, it's Pa-tri-cia! Heav-en, that's where you'll be when she's in your arms! Who took the place of De De Di-nah? Pa-tri-cia! And Peg-gy Sue is jeal-ous,

too, of Pa - tri - cia! And when she's wear-ing her bi - ki - ni,

Her hips will have you hyp - no - tized!

Far off in Ja - pan, they brag a - bout their Gei - sha,

Who cares, 'long as Un - cle Sam has got Pa -

charms._____ Far off
in Ja - pan, they brag a - bout their Gei - sha,
Who cares, 'long as Un - cle Sam has got Pa - tri cia!
tri - cia!

PERHAPS, PERHAPS, PERHAPS

English lyrics by Joe Davis
Spanish lyrics and music by Osvaldo Farres

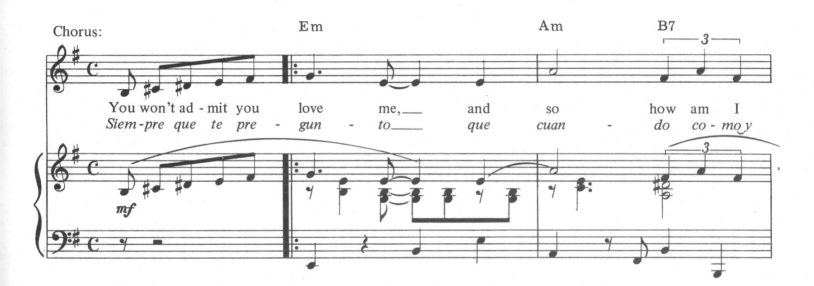

Chorus:

You won't ad - mit you love me,___ and so how am I
Siem -pre que te pre - gun - to___ que cuan - do co - mo y

ev - er___ to know? You al - ways tell me,___ Per -
don - de,___ tú siem - pre me res - pon - des___ Qui -

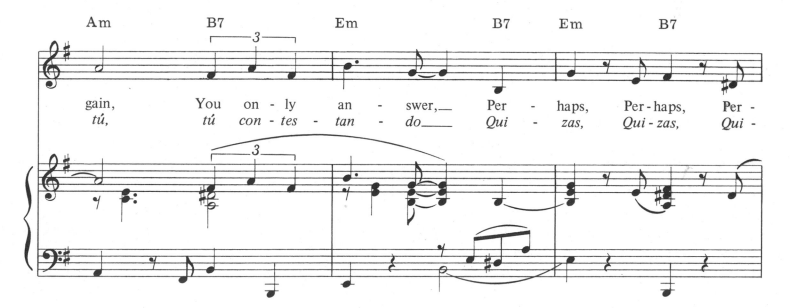

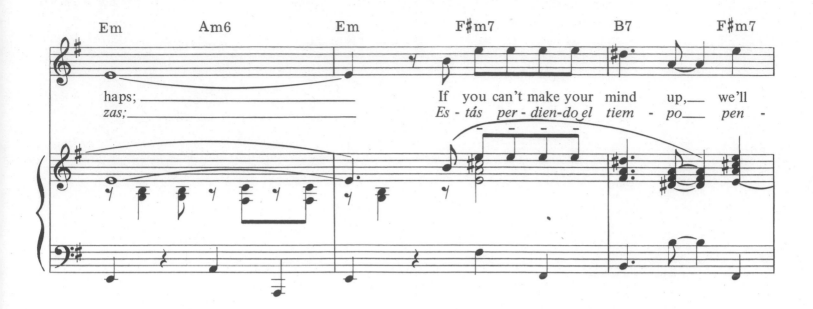

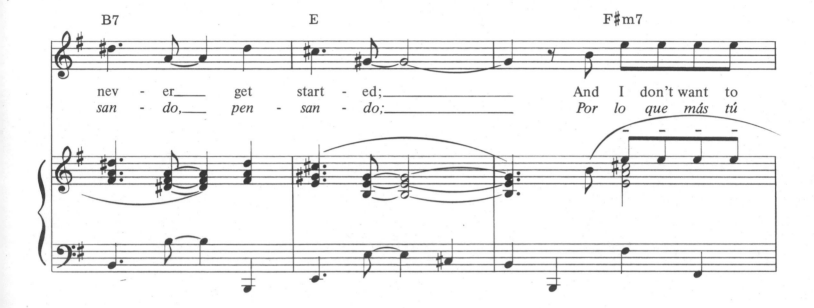

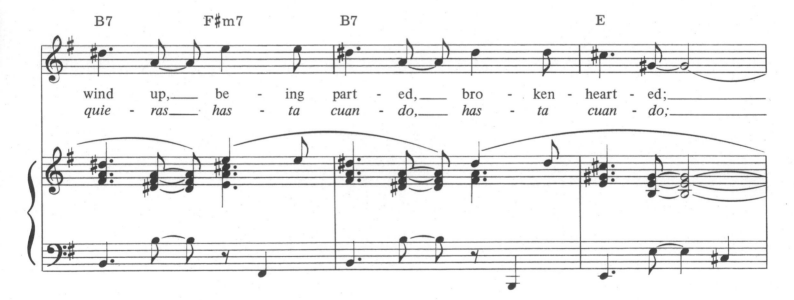

224

THE PEANUT VENDOR

English lyrics by Marion Sunshine and L. Wolfe Gilbert
Spanish lyrics and music by Moises Simons

In Cu - ba,   each mer - ry maid   wakes up with
In Cu - ba,   his smil - ing face   is wel - come

this ser - e - nade: Pea - nuts!_____ They're nice_ and hot,
most ev - 'ry place.   Pea - nuts!_____ They hear_ him cry,
                        *Ma - ni!*_____

Pea - nuts! _____ I sell _____ a lot.
Pea - nuts! _____ They all _____ re - ply.
Ma - ni! _____

If you have - n't got ba - nan - as, don't ___ be blue,
If you're look - ing for an ear - ly morn - ing treat,
Ca - se - ri - ta no te a - cues - tes a _____ dor - mir,

Pea - nuts in a lit - tle bag are call - ing you.
Get some dou - ble joint - ed pea - nuts good ___ to eat.
Sin co - mer - te un cu - cu - ru - cho de _____ ma - ní.

Don't waste them,   no tum - my ache,   you'll taste them
For break - fast   or din - ner time,   for sup - per,

when you __ a wake.   For at the ver - y break __ of day,
most an - y - time.   A mer - ry twin - kle in ___ his eye,
Que sa - bro - si - to y ri - co es - tá,
Cuan - do la ca - lle so __ la es - tá,

The pea - nut ven - dor's on __ his way. ___ At dawn - ing
He's got a way ___ that makes __ you buy. ___ Each morn - ing
Ya no se pue - de pe - dir más. ___
Ca - se - ra de ___ mi co - ra - zón. ___

that whis - tle blows, Through ev -'ry cit - y, town,___ and coun - try lane,
that whis - tle blows, The lit - tle chil - dren like___ to trail___ a - long,
Ay ca - se - ri - ta no___ me de - jes ir,
El ma - ni - se - ro en - to___ na su___ pre - gón,

You'll hear him sing his plain - tive lit - tle strain,
They love to hear the pea - nut ven - dor's song.
Por - que des - pués te vas___ a - rre - pen - tir,
Y si la ni - ña es - cu - cha mi can - tar,

And as he goes by,___ to you___ he'll say:___ Big Jum - bo's,
They all laugh with glee___ when he___ will say:___ They're roast - ed,
Y va a ser muy tar - de ya.___
Lla - ma des - de su___ bal - cón.___

Big dou - ble ones, come buy those Pea - nuts roast - ed to - day,___
no ti - ny ones, they're roast - ed, Pea - nuts hot in the shell,___
Ma - ni - se - ro se va,___
Da - me de tu ma - ni,___

___ Come try those Fresh - ly roast - ed to - day!___ If you're look - ing for a
___ Come buy some, I eat more than I sell!___ If an ap - ple keeps the
___ *Ma - ni - se - ro se va,___ Ca - se - ri - ta no te a*
___ *Da - me de tu ma - ni,___ Que es - ta no - che no voy*

mor - al to ___ his song, Fif - ty mil - lion lit - tle mon - keys can't ___ be wrong.
doc - tor from ___ your door, Pea - nuts ought to keep him from you ev - er - more.
cues - tes a ___ dor - mir sin co - mer - te un cu - cu - ru - cho de ___ ma - ni.
a po - der ___ dor - mir sin co - mer - me un cu - cu - ru - cho de ___ ma - ni.

230

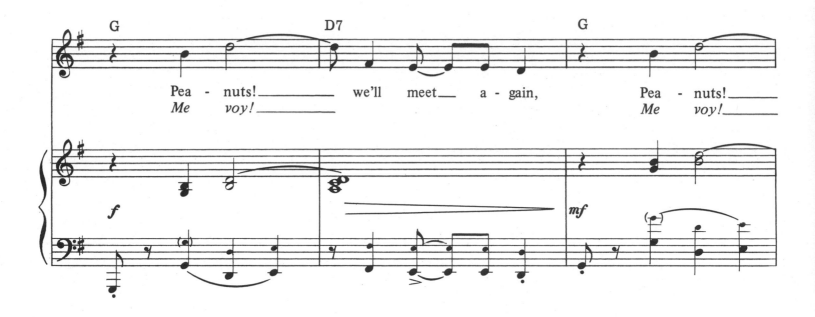

Pea - nuts!_____ we'll meet____ a - gain,   Pea - nuts!_____
*Me voy!*_____   *Me voy!*_____

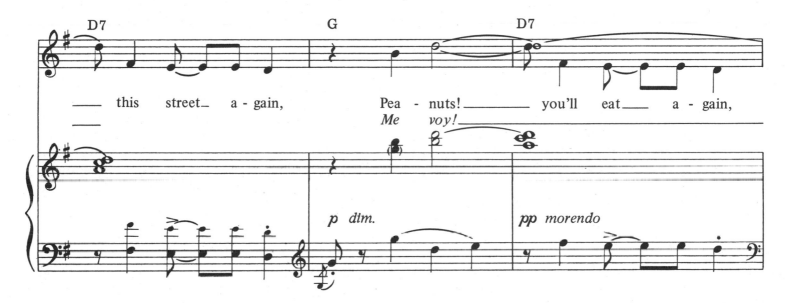

_____ this street____ a - gain,   Pea - nuts!_____ you'll eat____ a - gain,
                                    *Me voy!*_____

your pea - nut man,   That pea - nut man's gone.

EL RANCHO GRANDE

English lyrics by Bartley Costello
Spanish lyrics and music by Silvano R. Ramos

rop - ing and a ty - ing, I'm rop - ing and a ty - ing.
le - gre me de - cí - a, Que a - le - gre me de - cí - a.

rit.

Verse:

1. Give me my ranch and my cat - tle,
2. Give me my bri - dle and sad - dle,
Te voy ha - cer tus cal - zo - nes,

a tempo

Far from the great cit - y's rat - tle;
And my old pin - to I'll strad - dle;
Co - mo los u - sa el ran - che - ro;

Give me a big herd to bat - tle, For I just
I'll get the cow - boys a - rid - ing, Out where the
Te los co - mien - zo de la - na, Te los a -

233

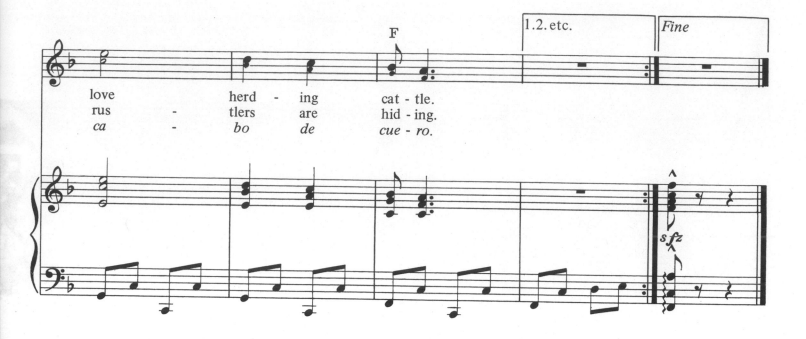

love   herd - ing   cat - tle.
rus -   tlers   are   hid - ing.
ca -   *bo*   *de*   *cue - ro.*

3rd Verse

Some-times the winter storms tearing,	*Nunca te fies de promesas*
Set all the cattle a-raring,	*Ni mucho menos de amores*
But when the winter is over,	*Que si te dan calabazas*
We're sure enough in the clover.	*Verás lo que son ardores.*

4th Verse

Give me the wide open spaces,	*Pon muy atento el oído*
That's just where I know my place is,	*Cuando rechine la puerta*
I love the Ro-de-o dearly,	*Hay muertos que no hacen ruido*
And the Big Round-Up yearly.	*Y son muy gordas sus penas.*

5th Verse

Tho' we play seven eleven,	*Cuando te pidan cigarro*
My Ranch is next door to Heaven,	*No des cigarro y cerillo*
We smile when we take a beatin',	*Porque si das las dos cosas*
But hang a rat when he's cheatin'.	*Te tantearán de zorrillo.*

PEREZ PRADO

SALAMANCA

ERNESTO LECUONA and ETHEL SMITH

SAY "SI SI"

English lyrics by Al Stillman and Francia Luban
Spanish lyrics and music by Ernesto Lecuona

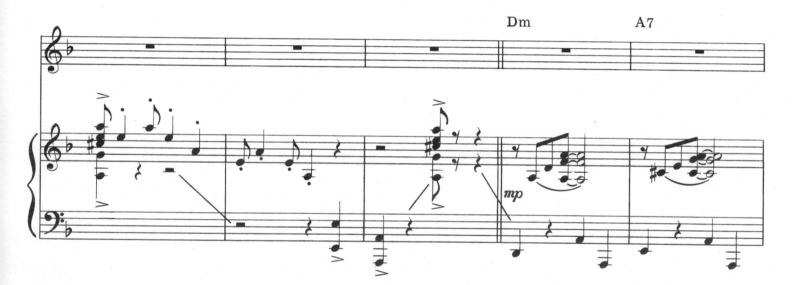

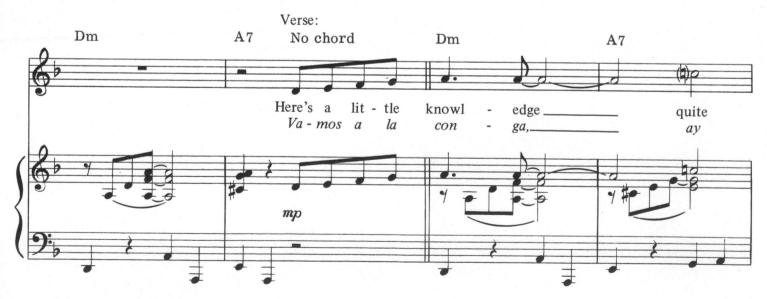

Here's a lit - tle knowl - edge _____ quite
Va - mos a la con - ga, _____ ay

good. _____ May-be it won't help you, _____ but it
Dios. _____ Va-mos que ya sue - na, _____ el bon-

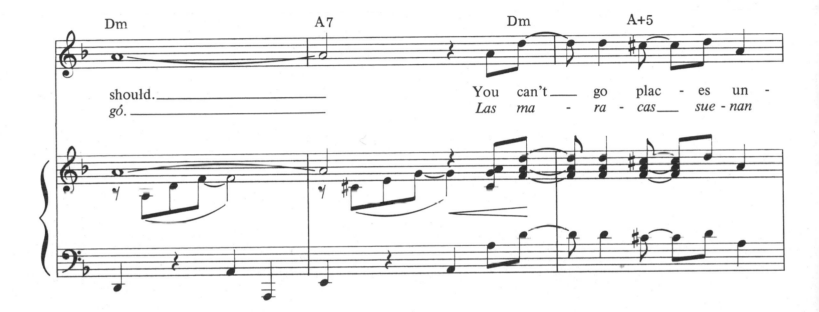

should. _____ You can't go plac - es un -
gó. _____ Las ma - ra - cas sue - nan

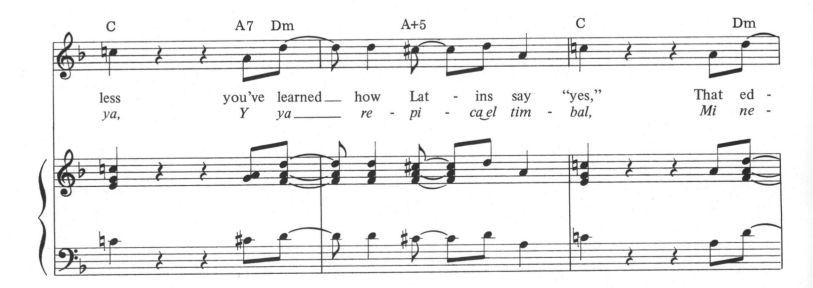

less you've learned how Lat - ins say "yes," That ed -
ya, Y ya re - pi - ca el tim - bal, Mi ne -

-u - ca - tion-al, in-spi - ra - tion-al, most sen - sa - tion-al "Yes."
-gra va - mos de - tras, ay que ya la con-ga no vuel-ve más.

Chorus:

In Spain they Say "Si, Si;" In
In Hin - du - stan "Ug! Ug;" Means
Pa - ra Vi - go me voy, Mi

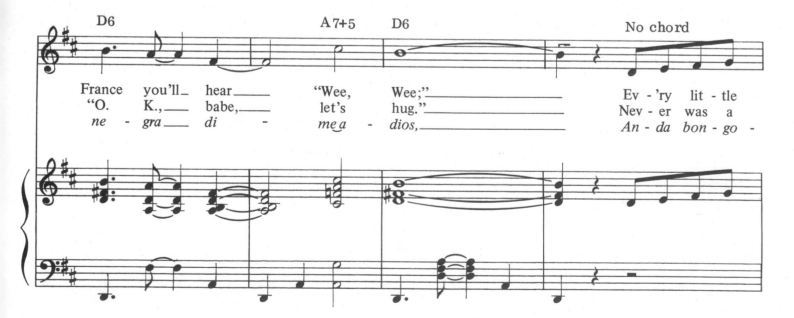

France you'll hear "Wee, Wee;" Ev - 'ry lit - tle
"O. K., babe, let's hug." Nev - er was a
ne - gra di - me a - dios, An - da bon - go-

238

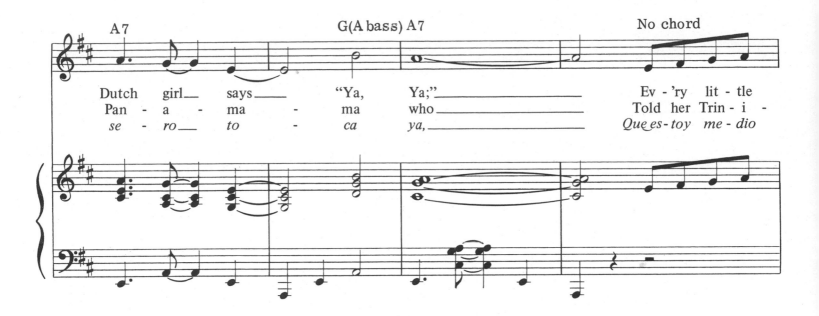

Dutch girl says____ "Ya, Ya;"_____ Ev - 'ry lit - tle
Pan - a - ma - ma who_____ Told her Trin - i -
se - ro____ to - ca ya,_____ Que es - toy me - dio

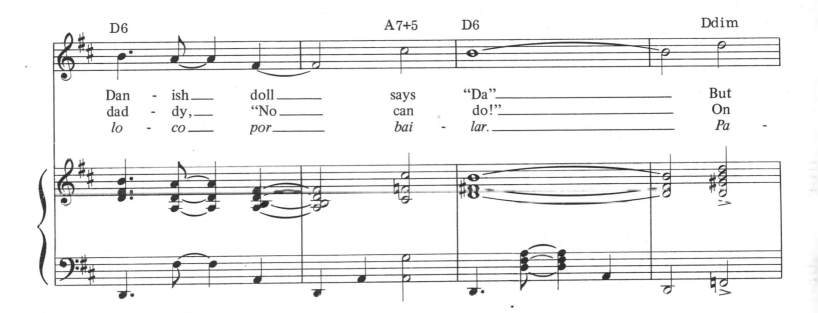

Dan - ish____ doll_____ says "Da"_____ But
dad - dy,____ "No_____ can do!"_____ On
lo - co____ por bai - lar._____ Pa -

sweet - heart____ tell_____ me why,_____ No
ev - 'ry____ Vir - gin Isle_____ They
ra Vi - go____ me voy,_____ Mi

239

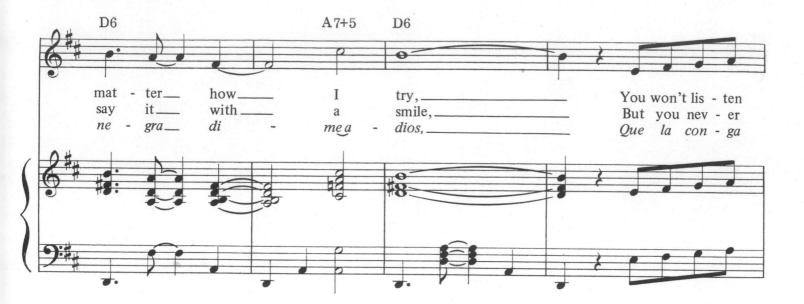

mat - ter___ how___ I try,_____ You won't lis - ten
say it with___ a smile,_____ But you nev - er
ne - gra___ di - me a - dios,_____ Que la con - ga

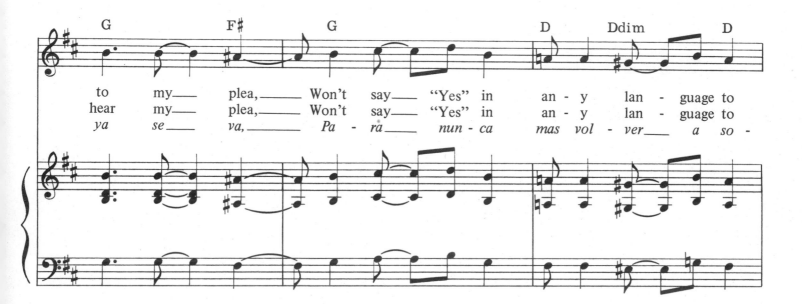

to my___ plea,___ Won't say___ "Yes" in an - y lan - guage to
hear my___ plea,___ Won't say___ "Yes" in an - y lan - guage to
ya se___ va,___ Pa - ra___ nun - ca mas vol - ver___ a so -

me. When will you___ Say_____ "Si, Si?"_____
me. When will you___ Say_____ "Si, Si?"_____
nar. Pa - ra Vi - go___ me voy.___

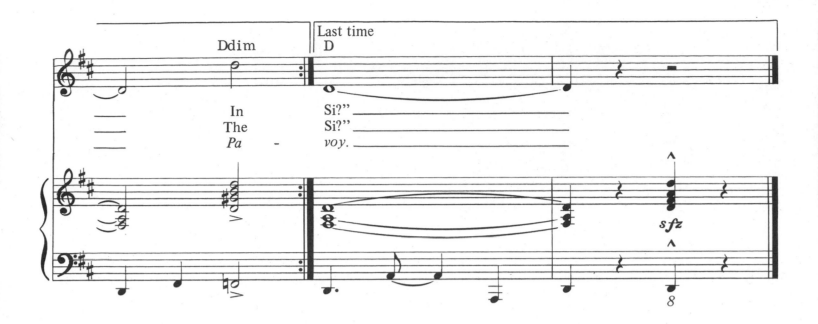

3rd Chorus

The monkeys in the tree
Don't have to say: "Si, Si;"
All they do is wag their little tails;
That's a little gag that never fails.
In darkest Africa
The natives say: "Uh, Huh!"
But you never hear my plea,
Won't say "Yes" in any language to me.
When will you Say "Si, Si?"

4th Chorus

Out West they say: "Wah Hoo!"
That's "O.K., Toots" to you.
Every Southern lady knows her stuff,
'Cause her answer always is "Sho Nuff!"
But, sweetheart, tell me why,
No matter how I try,
You won't listen to my plea,
Won't say "Yes" in any language to me.
When will you Say "Si, Si?"

5th Chorus

In Washington, D.C.,
The yes-men say: "Si, Si;"
There are lots of politicians, though
Who can always say both "Yes" and "No."
But, sweetheart, tell me why,
No matter how I try,
You won't listen to my plea,
Won't say "Yes" in any language to me.
When will you Say "Si, Si?"

6th Chorus

A lady horse, they say,
Means "Yes" when she says: "Neigh!"
Every little gal from Mexico
Hates to give a pal a "No, No, No!"
So, sweetheart, tell me why,
No matter how I try,
You won't listen to my plea,
Won't say "Yes" in any language to me.
When will you Say "Si, Si?"

7th Chorus

In 606 B.C.,
Those gals would mix, Si, Si!
Every little cave man used his dome,
Hit 'em on the head, then dragged 'em home.
So, sweetheart, tell me why,
No matter how I try,
You won't listen to my plea,
Won't say "Yes" in any language to me.
When will you Say "Si, Si?"

THE STORY OF LOVE

English lyrics by George Thorn
Spanish lyrics and music by Carlos Almaran

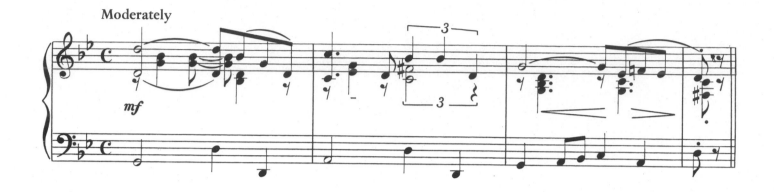

Chorus:

All at once you find your dreams are com-ing true_____ and you won-der what is
Ya no_es-tás más a mi la-do co-ra-zón,_____ en el al-ma só-lo

hap-pen-ing to you!_____ Then you feel your head go spin-ning, but it's on-ly the be-
ten-go so-le-dad y si yo no pue-do ver-te, ¿Por qué Dios me hi-zo que-

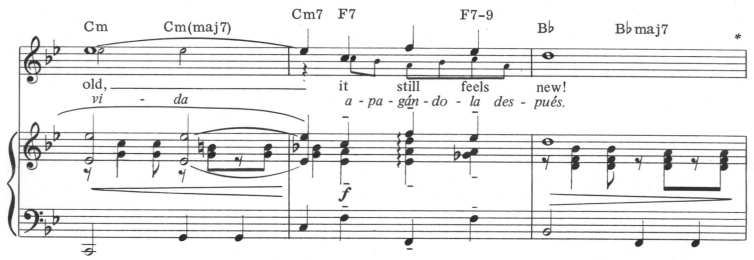

*N.B.: For English version cut from * (asterisk) to * (asterisk).*

UN TELEGRAMA

Lyrics and music by Garcia Segura

Moderately

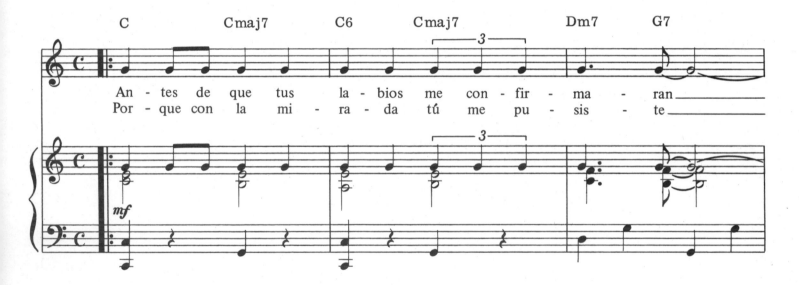

An - tes de que tus la - bios me con - fir - ma - ran _____
Por - que con la mi - ra - da tú me pu - sis - te _____

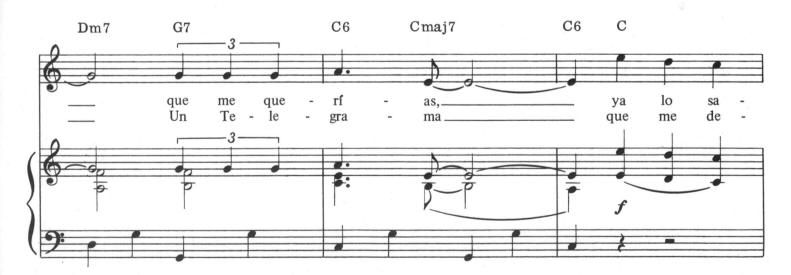

_____ que me que - rí - as, _____ ya lo sa -
_____ Un Te - le - gra - ma _____ que me de -

Tico-Tico

English lyrics by Ervin Drake
Portuguese lyrics by Aloysio Oliveira
Music by Zequinha Abreu

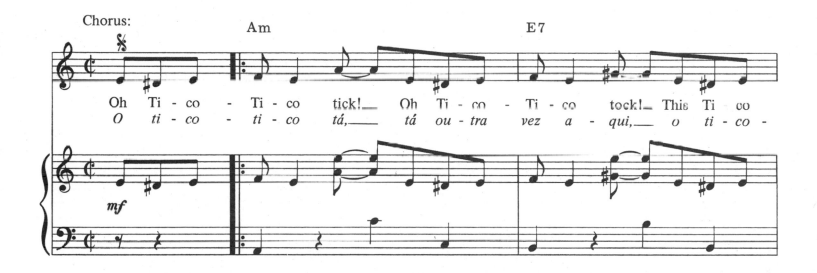

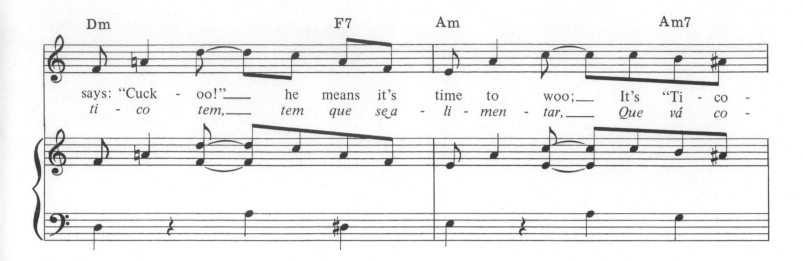

says: "Cuck - oo!"___ he means it's time to woo;___ It's "Ti - co -
ti - co tem,___ tem que se a - li - men - tar,___ Que vá co -

time" for all the lov - ers in the block. I've got a
mer u - mas mi - nho - cas no po - mar. O ti - co -

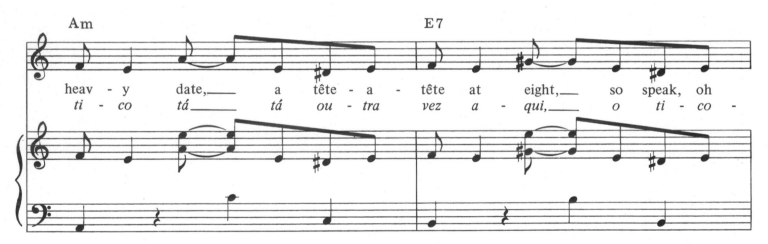

heav - y date,___ a tête - a - tête at eight,___ so speak, oh
ti - co tá___ tá ou - tra vez a - qui,___ o ti - co -

Ti - co, tell me is it get - ting late? If I'm on time:"Cuck-oo!"___ but if I'm
ti - co tá co - men - do o meu fu - bá. Eu sei que el - le vem___ vi - ver no

late, "Woo - woo!"__ The one my heart has gone to may not want to
meu quin - tal,___ e vem com a - res de ca - há - rio e de par -

wait! For just a bird - ie, and a bird - ie who goes no-where, He knows of
dal. Mas por fa - vor ti - ra es - se bi - cho do ce - lei - ro, por-que el-le a -

ev - 'ry Lov-ers' Lane and how to go there; For in af - fairs of the heart,_ my Ti - co's
ca - ba co-men-do o fu - bá in - tei - ro. Ti - ra es - se ti - co de lá,___ de ci - ma

ter - ri - bly smart,_ He tells me: "Gent-ly, sen - ti - men-t'ly at the start!" Oh-oh, I
do meu fu - bá.___ Tem tan - ta fru - ta que el-le po - de pi - ni - car. Eu já fiz

hear my lit-tle Ti-co-Ti-co call-ing, Be-cause the time is right and shades of night are

tu-do pa-ra ver se con-se-gui-a. Bo-tei al-pis-te pa-ra ver si el-le co-

C   **F**   **Cdim**   **C**   (Optional)

fall - ing.   I love that not - so - cuck-oo cuck-oo in the clock: Ti - co -

mi - a. Bo-tei um ga-to um es-pan-ta-lho e um al-ça - pão, mas el-le a-cha que o fu-

Dm   **G7**   1. **C**   No chord   2. *To next strain* **C**   *Fine* **C**

Ti-co-Ti-co Ti-co-Ti-co tock. Oh, Ti-co- tock._____ tock._____

bá é que é bo-a a-li-men-ta - ção. O ti-co- ção._____ ção._____

sfz mf   *sfz*

Interlude:

Touch the Wind

Lyrics and music by Juan Carlos Calderon and Mike Hawker

I woke up this morn - ing,   and my
Co - mo u - na pro - me - sa,   e - res

mind fell a - way,
tú,   e - res tú.

Look - ing back sad - ly   from to - mor - row.
Co - mo u - na ma - ña - na   de ve - ra - no.

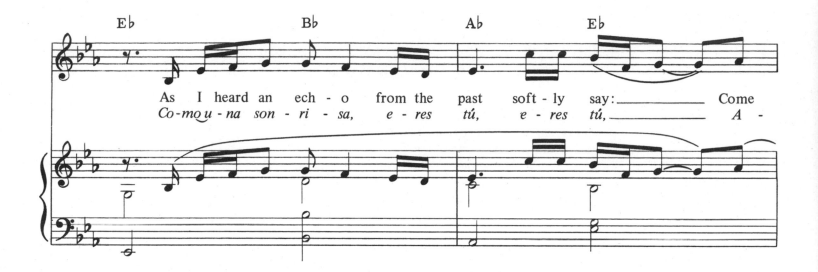

As I heard an ech-o from the past soft-ly say:_____ Come
Co-mo u-na son-ri-sa, e-res tú, e-res tú,_____ A-

back,_____ come back, won't you stay?
sí,_____ a-sí, e-res tú.

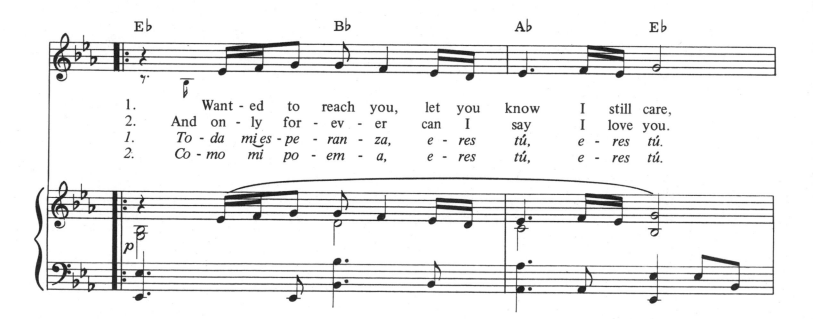

1.   Want-ed to reach you, let you know I still care,
2. And on-ly for-ev-er can I say I love you.
1. *To-da mi es-pe-ran-za, e-res tú, e-res tú.*
2. *Co-mo mi po-em-a, e-res tú, e-res tú.*

Bb **Ab** **Bb**

I'm lost in the si - lence of my sor - row.
And on - ly for - ev - er have I lost you.
Co - mo llu - via fres - ca en mis ma - nos.
Co - mo_u - na gui - ta - rra en la no - che.

Eb **Bb** **Ab** **Eb** **Ab**

And I put a prom - ise in the wind, on the air, _____ to
But on - ly a dream - er could wake up, as I do, _____ and
Co - mo fuer - te bri - sa, e - res tú, e - res tú, _____ a -
Co - mo mi ho - ri - zon - te, e - res tú, e - res tú, _____ a -

Eb (Bb bass) **Bb 7sus4** **Eb** **Ab (Bb bass)** **Eb** **Bb (D bass)**

fly _____ a - way to you there. }
hope _____ it's still yes - ter - day. }
sí, _____ a - sí, e - res tú. }
sí, _____ a - sí, e - res tú. }

Touch The

E - res

258

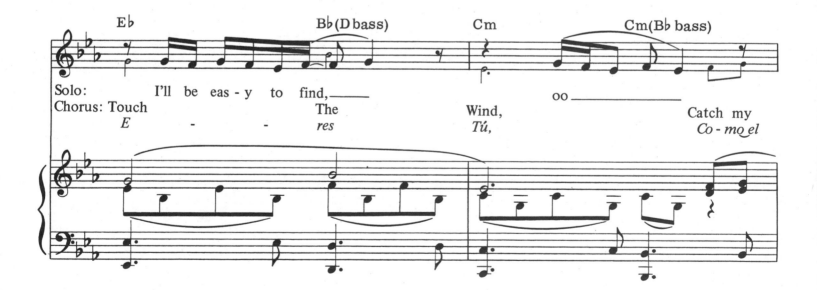

WHEN THE LIGHTS ARE SOFT AND LOW

English lyrics by Bert Child
Music by E. Donato

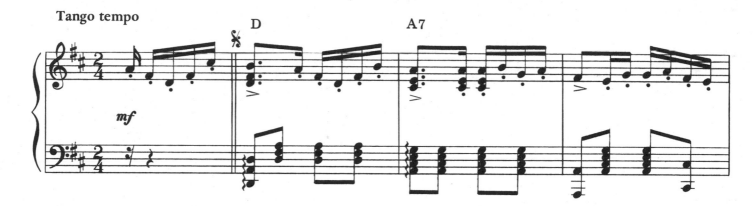

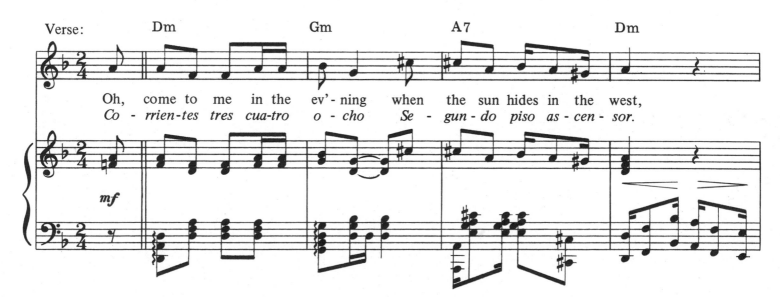

Verse:

Oh, come to me in the ev'-ning when the sun hides in the west,
Co - rrien-tes tres cua-tro o - cho Se - gun-do piso as - cen-sor.

I am ev-er of you dream-ing_____ when at night I go to rest. Oh,
No hay por-te-ros ni ve - ci - nos_____ A- den-tro cock-tail y a- mor Pi -

come to my arms, my loved one,_____ Clasp me to your arms so dear. The
si - to que pu - so Ma - ple;_____ Pia - no es-te - ra y ve - la - dor. Un

stars will pro-tect you, sweet one,_____ Please tell that you will be mine, dear,
te - le - fón que con - tes - te_____ U - na vic-tro-la que llo - ra

We will dance un-til the dawn, till the sun comes in the morn, and the shades of night will be gone.
Vie-jos tan-gos de mi flor y un ga - to de por-ce - la - na pa' que no mau-lle el a-mor.

2	II
Each dew-drop tells me a story	*Juncal doce veinticuatro,*
As it rests upon the grass	*Telefonea sin temor,*
I am always in my glory	*De tarde, té con masitas,*
When thru open fields I pass.	*De noche, tango y cantar.*
A story of love each tells me	*Los domingos, té danzante*
That you will be ever true,	*Los lunes, desolación;*
It is then that I am carefree	*Hay de todo en la casita:*
Knowing that I will be near you.	*Almohadones y divanes*
May our love, dear, never end	*Como en boticas, cocó,*
As thru life our way we wend	*Alfombras que no hacen ruido,*
And to heav'n this message we send:	*Y mesa puesto al amor.*
Chorus: When Lights Are Soft And Low,	*Chorus: Y todo a media luz,*
etc.	*etc.*

Vaya Con Dios

Lyrics and music by Larry Russell, Inez James and Buddy Pepper

Chorus:

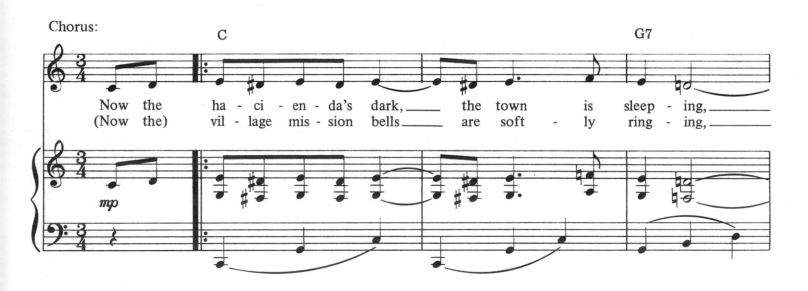

Now the ha - ci - en - da's dark,___ the town is sleep - ing,___
(Now the) vil - lage mis - sion bells___ are soft - ly ring - ing,___

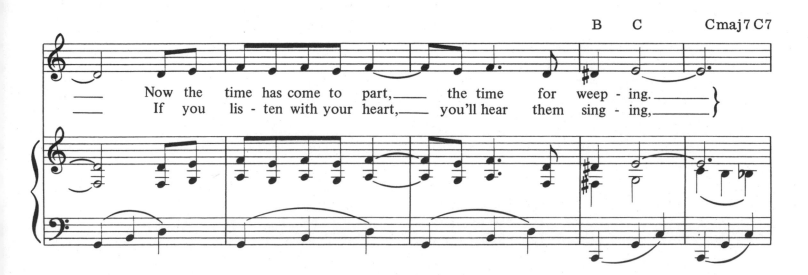

___ Now the time has come to part,___ the time for weep - ing.___
___ If you lis - ten with your heart,___ you'll hear them sing - ing,___

Va - ya Con Di - os, my dar - ling,_____ May God be with you, my love._____ Now the

1. with you, my love._____ Wher -

2. C Dm7 C

ev - er you may be,_____ I'll be be - side you,_____ Al -

though you're man - y mil - lion dreams a - way._____ Each

night I'll say a pray'r,___ a pray'r to guide you,___ To

has-ten ev-'ry lone-ly hour of ev-'ry lone-ly day. Now the

poco rit.

dawn is break-ing through___ a gray to-mor-row,___ But the

a tempo

mem - o - ries we share___ are there to bor - row.___

Va - ya Con Di - os, my dar - ling,___

May God be with you, my love.___

poco a poco rit.

p

WHAT A DIFFERENCE A DAY MADE

English lyrics by Stanley Adams
Spanish lyrics and music by Maria Grever

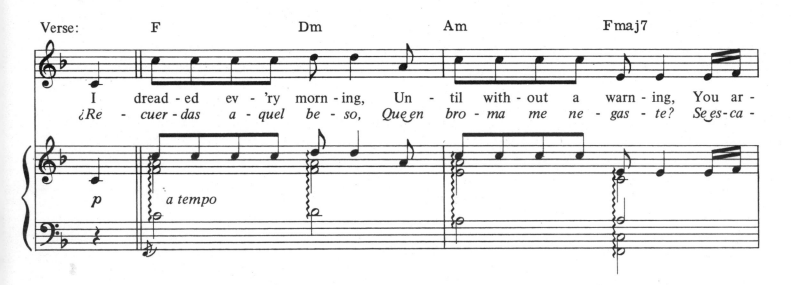

I dread-ed ev-'ry morn-ing, Un-til with-out a warn-ing, You ar-
¿Re - cuer - das a - quel be - so, Que en bro - ma me ne - gas - te? Se es - ca-

rived bring-ing heav-en to my door.
And you changed all my blue notes to a
pó de tus la - bios sin que - rer.
A - sus - ta - do por e - llo bus - có a-

WITHOUT YOU

English lyrics by Ray Gilbert
Spanish lyrics and music by Osvaldo Farres

Chorus:

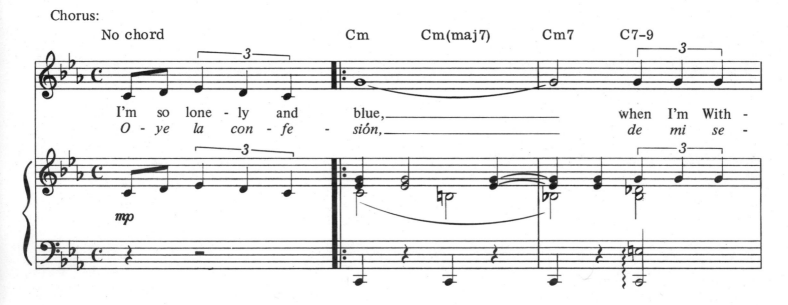

I'm so lone - ly and blue, _____ when I'm With -
O - ye la con - fe - sión, _____ de mi se -

out You, _____ I don't know what I'd do, _____
cre - to, _____ Na - ce de un co - ra - zón _____

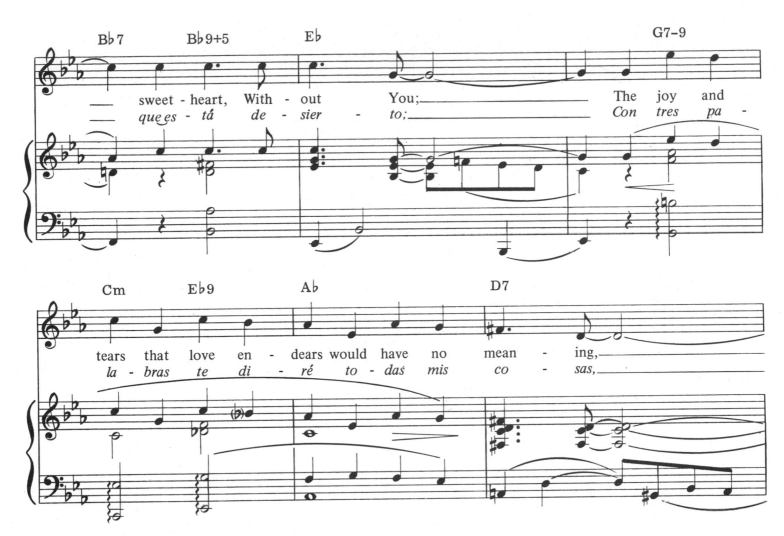

Bb7 Bb9+5 Eb G7-9

sweet - heart, With - out You; The joy and
que es - tá de - sier - to; Con tres pa -

Cm Eb9 Ab D7

tears that love en - dears would have no mean - ing,
la - bras te di - ré to - das mis co - sas,

Fm Fm6 Ab7

3
If I did - n't have you to keep me
Co - sas del co - ra - zón que son pre -

Fm6 G7 No chord Cm Cm(maj7)

3
dream - ing; At the close of each day
cio - sas; Da - me tus ma - nos, ven

3

when I'm With - out You,_____ And my heart kneels to
to - ma las mi - as,_____ que te voy a con -

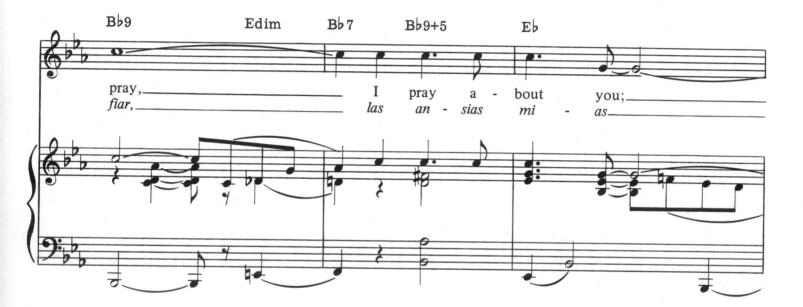

pray,_____ I pray a - bout you;_____
fiar,_____ las an - sias mi - as_____

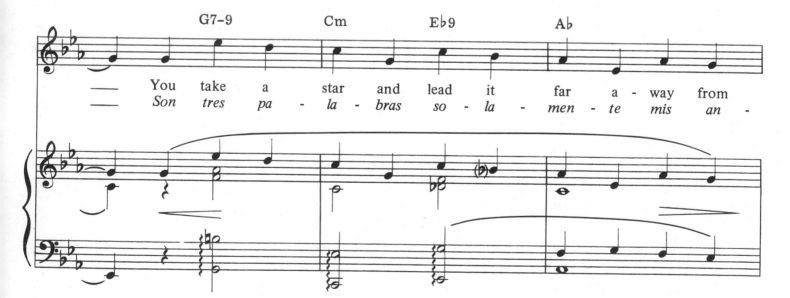

You take a star and lead it far a - way from
Son tres pa - la - bras so - la - men - te mis an -

You Belong To My Heart

English lyrics by Ray Gilbert
Spanish lyrics and music by Agustin Lara

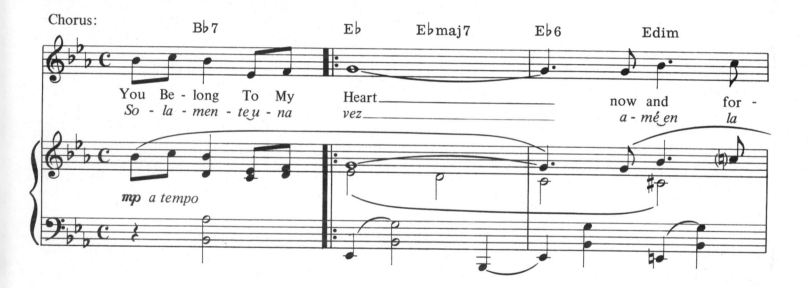

You Be-long To My Heart_____ now and for-
So - la - men - te u - na vez_____ a - mé en la

ev - er,_____ And our love had its start_____
vi - da,_____ so - la - men - te u - na vez

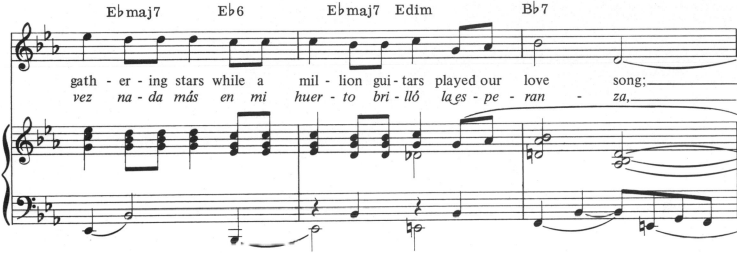

do you re - mem - ber?_____ And your eyes threw a

se en-tre - ga el al - ma,_____ con la dul - ce y to -

kiss_____ when they met mine;_____

tal_____ re - nun - cia - ción._____

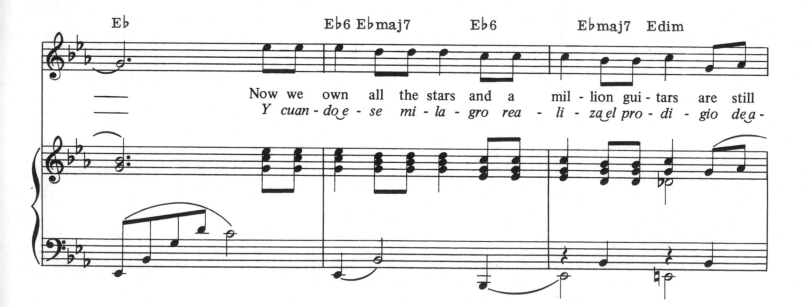

Now we own all the stars and a mil - lion gui - tars are still

Y cuan-do e - se mi - la - gro rea - li - za el pro - di - gio de a -

play - ing; _____
mar - se, _____

Dar - ling, you are the song and you'll
hay cam - pa - nas de fies - ta que

1.

al - ways be - long to my heart.
can - tan en el co - ra - zón.

You Be - long To My
So - la - men - te u - na

2.

al - ways be - long to my heart. _____
can - tan en el co - ra - zón. _____

poco rit.

L.H.

p

YOURS

English lyrics by Albert Gamse and Jack Sherr
Spanish lyrics by Agustin Rodriguez
Music by Gonzalo Roig

1. This night has mu - sic, the sweet - est
2. (The cloak of) eve - ning is wrapped a -
Quié - re - me mu - cho dul - ce a - mor

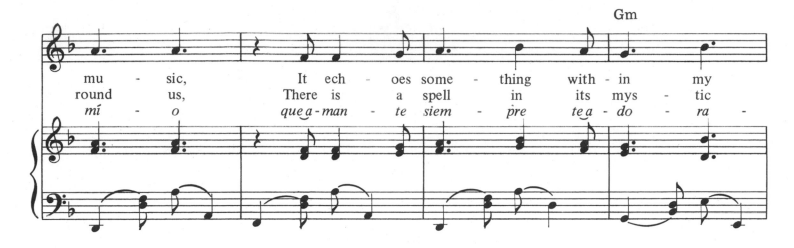

mu - sic,   It ech - oes some - thing with - in my
round us,   There is a spell in its mys - tic
mí - o   que a - man - te siem - pre te a - do - ra -

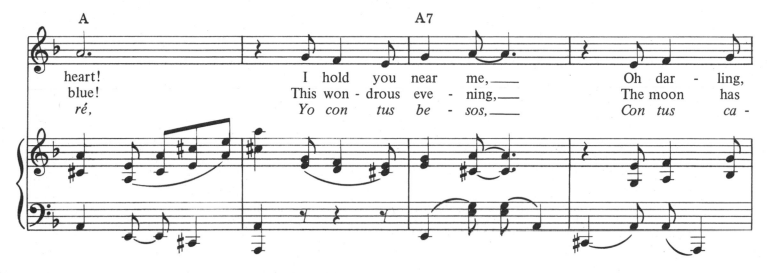

heart!   I hold you near me, ___   Oh dar - ling,
blue!   This won - drous eve - ning, ___   The moon has
ré,   Yo con tus be - sos, ___   Con tus ca -

hear me, ___   I have a mes - sage   I must im -
found us, ___   It hears me of - fer   my all to
ri - cias, ___   Mis su - fri - mien - tos   a - ca - lla -

1.
part. ___   2. The cloak of you. ___
ré. ___   Quié - re - me ré. ___

Yours till the stars lose their glo-ry!
Cuan-do se quie-re de ve-ras,

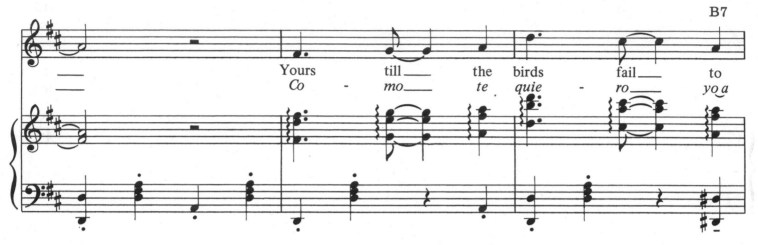

Yours till the birds fail to
Co-mo te quie-ro yo a

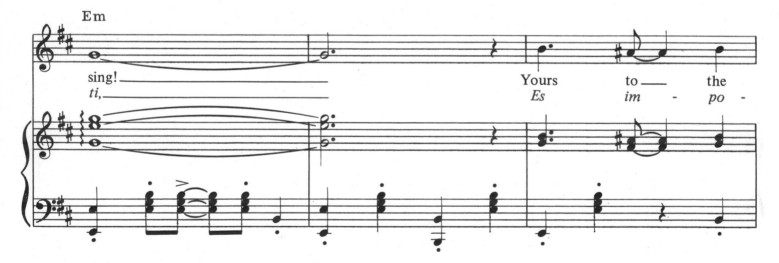

sing! Yours to the
ti, Es im-po-

end of life's sto-ry, This pledge to
si-ble mi cie-lo tan se-pa-

you, dear,_____ I bring!_____
ra - dos,_____ vi vir._____

_____ Yours in___ the gray of___ De -
_____ Cuan - do___ se quie - re___ de

cem - ber,_____ Here or___ on
ve - ras,_____ Co - mo___ te

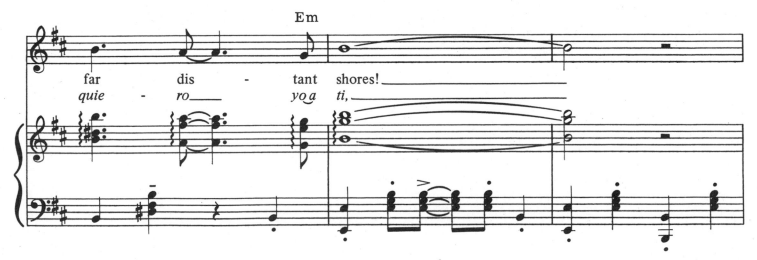

far dis - tant shores!_____
quie - ro___ yo a ti,_____

I've nev - er loved an - y one the way__ I love
es im - po - si - ble__ mi cie - lo tan__ se - pa -

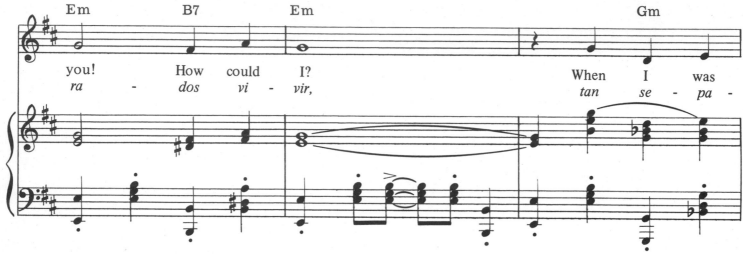

you! How could I? When I was
ra - dos vi - vir, tan se - pa -

born to be_____ just Yours.__
ra - dos_____ vi - vir.__

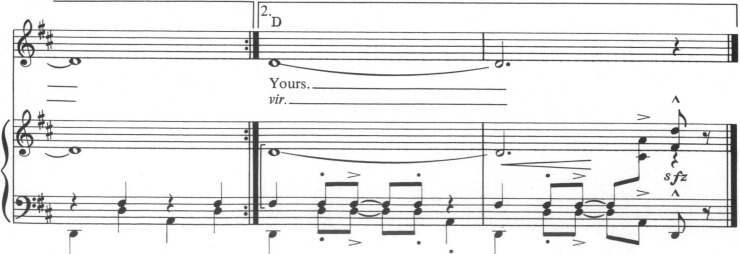

Yours.__
vir.__

Yesterday I Heard The Rain

English lyrics by Gene Lees
Music by A. Manzanero

Slowly, with expression

Chorus:

Yes - ter - day I Heard The Rain whis-per-ing your name, ask-ing where you'd gone.
Es - ta tar - de vi llo - ver, vi gen - te co - rrer y no es - ta - bas tú.

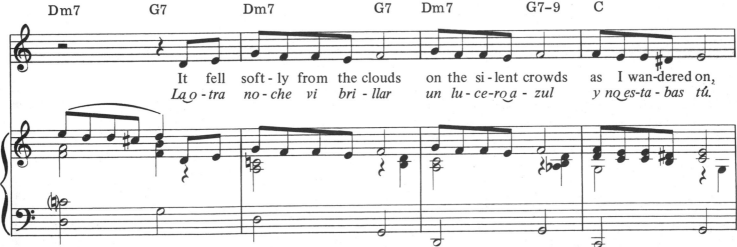

It fell soft - ly from the clouds on the si - lent crowds as I wan-dered on,
La o-tra no-che vi bri - llar un lu-ce-ro a-zul y no es-ta-bas tú.

Out of door-ways,__ black um - brel -las__ came to pur - sue me,
La o-tra tar - de__ vi que un a - ve__ e - na-mo - ra-da

Face -less peo - ple__ as they passed__ were look -ing
da - ba be - sos__ a su a - mor__ i - lu - sio -

through me,__ no one knew me.__ Yes - ter - day I shut my eyes,
na - da__ y no es - ta - bas.__ Es - ta tar - de vi llo - ver

face up to the skies, drink-ing in the rain, But your im-age still was there,
vi gen-te co-rrer y no es-ta-bas tú El o - to-ño vi lle-gar, al

LYRICISTS AND COMPOSERS